CATCH • THEM THINKING • IN SOCIAL STUDIES

Michael Hickman
and
Erin O'Donnell Wigginton

Foreword by Tim Erickson

SkyLight
Training and Publishing Inc.

Catch Them Thinking in Social Studies

Published by SkyLight Training and Publishing Inc.
2626 S. Clearbrook Dr., Arlington Heights, IL 60005-5310
800-348-4474 or 847-290-6600
Fax 847-290-6609
info@iriskylight.com
http://www.iriskylight.com

Senior Vice President, Product Development: Robin Fogarty
Director, Product Development: Ela Aktay
Acquisitions Editor: Jean Ward
Editors: Martha White and Jill Oldham
Project Coordinator: Sue Schumer
Cover Designer and Illustrator: David Stockman
Book Designer: Bruce Leckie
Formatters: Donna Ramirez and Vicki Hargis
Production Supervisor: Bob Crump
Production Assistant: Christina Georgi
Proofreader: Jodi Keller
Indexer: Schroeder Indexing

ISBN 1-57517-144-9
LCCCN 98-61531

2380V
Item Number 1706
Z Y X W V U T S R Q P O N M L K J I H G F E D C B A
06 05 04 03 02 01   15 14 13 12 11 10 9 8 7 6 5 4 3 2

Contents

Foreword

I never expected to be writing a foreword to a social studies book. I'm a math guy. But I wrote two books for the math classroom, *Get It Together* and *United We Solve*, that feature problems in the same format that you will find here. In fact, the authors of this book claim in their introduction that my work helped inspire theirs, which is flattering, and I guess explains why they asked me.

But it's still odd when you think that social studies (and all the classes it changed into—you know, American history, civics, and all that) was always my very worst subject. It wasn't quite just dates and names by the time I went through school, but it still meant writing long reports that were mainly regurgitated encyclopedia entries. There were some rays of hope, however: in 1965, in seventh grade, we actually had a debate about the Vietnam war (we now forget that seventh-graders were generally for it at that time); and I had one teacher who, I now recognize, must have just attended a summer institute. She started us in September with a monstrous and detailed unit about a colony in New England, complete with maps of who lived where and did what. We had the chance to act like historians. I remember nothing of the unit but the impressions of cool maps and the teacher's realization in February that she had only just made it from 1620 to 1700—and that if she was going to reach the present by June, she had better get a move on.

Curiously, a similar phenomenon was taking place in the disconnected but parallel world of middle school/junior high school math. While the vast majority of teachers were still pounding facts and algorithms, a precious few had realized that there were alternatives to "drill and kill," and were finding out, painfully, that these alternatives in mathematics instruction were not very well developed.

One of these alternatives was group work. Working alone is isolating and frustrating, and not at all like the world outside the classroom. Of course, students need individual accountability, but we should devote some time to cooperation and communication in small groups—which sounds fine until you assign a semester project and tell the kids to work together. It's an invitation to chaos, recrimination, and disappointment. Why? Because cooperation is not an instinct: it must be learned. Fortunately, even inexperienced students can develop the behavioral norms and personal expectations that make cooperation work.

The many gurus of cooperative learning will tell you how to start developing that sense of community. And they will give you great team-building activities. But soon there comes a time when you have to return to the curriculum, and your students are not yet ready to do that term project in groups . . . which is where a book like this comes in.

The activities in *Catch Them Thinking in Social Studies* give students something to cooperate about. They feature what educational researchers David and Roger Johnson call "structural independence," that is, these activities are designed so that each group member has information essential to the group's success. Your students can finish most of these within a class period as they learn some facts and have a good time. More important, however, they'll develop process skills: skills in logical thinking and skills in communication and collaboration.

When I do workshops using cooperative math problems, teachers often say, "If I had learned math this way when I was young, I might have a done a lot better." I think I can safely make the corresponding claim about these activities: as an historically-impaired person, I bet I would have learned more, done better, and made the social sciences more a part of my life if I had had tools like these.

Tim Erickson, Ph.D.
Curriculum Developer, Mathematics

Preface

When I first shared the process of cooperative problem solving in social studies with my fellow colleague, teacher trainer Erin O'Donnell Wigginton, she could see my exuberance. We agreed we would try to develop a trial activity that we could use in her government classroom. In less than two weeks time, we did develop an activity and Erin used it in her class. She reported that it was a success.

Erin and I are both disciples of active learning. We believe in setting a table that affords our students the opportunity to think, to discover, and to learn.

The story of our book begins with my travels and experiences as a social studies department chairperson and teacher-trainer—as well as a former classroom teacher—who used cooperative learning strategies in the classroom. I had been looking for sessions that might benefit math classroom teachers in cooperative learning. In late 1996, while at a SERVE (South East Region Vision for Education) conference in Charlotte, North Carolina, I spied what I thought would be an interesting presentation. The session I chose to attend was being conducted by Dr. Tim Erickson of the University of California, Berkeley. When I walked in he greeted me and invited me to sit with a group of three other educators. I was a few minutes late to the session so I joined them when they were already underway with an activity.

There were at least eight tables with teams of four working diligently at a task. The members of my group handed me a card and told me that I was responsible for the information on that card. I had no idea what we were doing. I read the information on the card; it consisted of statements that provided some information—information that I would later discover was vital to solving the problem. However, my card did not contain all of the information that was needed to arrive at a solution. Each of the team members would have some data necessary to solve the problem as we organized, it was decided each member would take turns reading the information on his or her card. We now knew what the problem entailed and we proposed different ways to go about solving the problem; a method was proposed and before long we had arrived at the solution. We did two more problems that morning and, before I knew it, almost two hours had passed.

Now, I was with math teachers and I am a former social studies teacher, so I felt a little out of place, but I am not bashful so I spoke up at different times. I made suggestions to the group and I asked questions and I felt like I grew from the experience. At the same time I was thinking that this was a great strategy; something like this was needed in the social sciences.

Erin and I discussed the process and we worked to create a second activity and then a third, each time discussing the activity and the process as it unfolded in the classroom. I told Erin that I thought we could create a useful collection of these activities. She agreed and *Catch Them Thinking in Social Studies* is the result of our collaboration.

Acknowledgments

We would like to thank and give credit to Dr. Tim Erickson for the insight and the inspiration for the idea of this book. We also followed some of the format that he uses in his book, *United We Solve.*

We would also like to thank the others who contributed in some fashion to the creation of this book. Dr. Tom DeBolt, a former principal, and Dr. Bill Asbury, superintendent of the Pulaski County, Virginia school system. They not only strived for and demanded excellence but encouraged our school system and its personnel to grow professionally. We also say thanks to our fellow trainers who encouraged and supported, they being Beth Sattes, Jackie Walsh, Frank Kasik, and Karen Clymer.

At Pulaski County High School, we would like to thank our librarian, Theda Gilmore, who helped greatly with some of the research on some topics. Theda went above and beyond as she was relentless in finding information for us when we were stymied. Fran Shelton and Wayne Wooten are members of our math department who helped with the spreadsheet activities. Erin Wigginton's students provided the ideal laboratory subjects to carry on and perfect the experiments.

Finally, to our families: to my spouse, Marva Hickman, and to the children of our two families, Tristan Hickman, and Paige and Matthew Wigginton, we say thank you for putting up with our unannounced visits and late evening phone conversations.

Mickey Hickman

Erin O'Donnell Wigginton

Introduction

What Is Cooperative Problem Solving?

Cooperative problem solving is an active, cooperative, higher-thinking, and fun way to cover and generate interest in social studies materials. Students working in teams of four get information about a social studies topic in the guise of four clue cards labeled A, B, C, D. The information, which is actually the lesson, is vital to solving a problem or completing a task designated in the cards and also, occasionally, in the introductory material for the activity.

The information is distributed carefully, evenly and nonsequentially over the four clue cards, and it takes information found on all four cards to solve the problem. Information contained on one, two, or three of the cards will not suffice. In many activities, vital information is also included in the Background Information part of an activity page.

To ensure participation by all members of the group, insist that the following rule be observed: Students are not to share information by physically passing their cards to other members of the group. Everyone must speak up and present his or her own information verbally. Everyone has at least one vital clue to which the other team members need to pay attention.

Not all information contained on the cards is vital to solving the problem. Some facts are not needed to solve the problem, yet may illuminate it in some way. Although clue information is always factual, some clues may be diversionary. So, in addition to working through solving a task, students have to sort through and organize the data and sometimes delete a red herring or two—much like in real life.

Students work only in teams. All the activities in this book are designed for teams of four (although other numbers could work depending on the adaptability of the teacher and the students). Teams can be set permanently, for a short term, or daily, and they can be put together simply by numbering off in class. Teachers should refrain from interjection information or directions.

A big part of the process is to let the students determine the course of action(s) to be taken. They will work together, make suggestions, use trial and error, negotiate through the process, and have a good time while they work together.

About the Activities in This Book

These activities are meant to be lifelike or have bearing on the real world in two ways. First, life does not always guarantee an answer, and there is not always someone on hand to give assistance. Second, in life all of the information that one receives is not useful or necessary to solve a problem.

Carefully structured and researched (see References at the end of this introduction), the activities in *Catch Them Thinking in Social Studies* place the students in role simulations based on history and drawn from social studies in general. By placing the students into a role simulation, you will find they learn to think and work with purpose. Students will have a goal in mind and a slant or perspective on their thinking. This slant helps guide and direct their work as they sort the data, analyze it, and create and test solutions.

The activities create problems for the student to solve. Problem solving requires a process similar to the following:

First, one must identify and comprehend the problem.

Second, the problem must be analyzed and resources and data gathered.

Third, the potential solution or plan(s) is conceived and selected.

Fourth, the plan is executed.

Fifth, the plan is interpreted and evaluated in terms of how well the plan or solution works.

As the students work through the activities, they will discover and develop a model for problem solving. They will also develop problem solving strategies such as trial and error (also called guess and check), working backwards, looking for a pattern, making an organizational list, using logical reasoning, and making a model, graph, or table.

How to Create Your Own Cooperative Problem Activity

As you use these activities in this book and become more familiar with how the process works, you may wish to customize the activities for your classwork. Following are directions on creating your own cooperative problem solving activities. By following these eight steps, any teacher in any discipline can create a cooperative problem solving activity:

1. Fix your purpose. Do your want to introduce or conclude a subject unit, supplement your instruction, or bridge from one topic to a seemingly unrelated one?

2. Decide what is to be taught and what is to be learned.

3. Define the end product of your activity. It should be something students can create or complete to illustrate the comprehension of a subject area. End products can be charts, tables, time lines, a plan, the answers to a set of questions, the solution to a mystery, a new or reconstructed statement, etc.

4. Assemble the information essential for arriving at the solution or finishing the end product. This information provides the text for the clues cards. This is the "duck-in-a-row" stage. (Spice up the material with teachable moments that help students learn about the topic. The information is not vital to solving the problem, but is more than "filler.")

5. Divide the information/clues evenly over the four cards. Take special care that each of the four contains information vital needed to the solution. By doing so, you ensure every team member's participation and relevance to the team. Be sure to arrange the information randomly on the individual cards so students cannot detect a sequence.

6. Now work through the problem yourself to check the accuracy of the information on the cards and whether you included all information to complete the task or solve the problem.

7. Write the introduction and background information for the activity. Your introduction may include the assignment of the task itself or some information needed to complete the task. You may or may not choose to advise students of this. Let it become a pleasant discovery at some point in the process.

8. Anticipate some students having difficulty working with the data and solving the problem. Prepare some hints that may aid less capable or younger students in the process. Capable students should be given the opportunity to figure out the problem for themselves.

Instructional Tips

In the cooperative problem solving process used in *Catch Them Thinking in Social Studies,* students should receive an envelope or folder with the problem, instructions, and the information needed to solve the problem or complete the task, usually found in the clue cards for the given activity. If an information page (Background Information), a map, or a chart goes with the activity, the teacher may want to photocopy and distribute that page first. The clue cards in this book are designed so that the teacher may reproduce the clues and then cut them into four pieces (A, B, C, D). An activity is best handled in class by putting the clue cards into an individual envelope for each group or team. Be sure to collect the cards at the end of the session for use at another time.

Allow time for the students to digest information on their clue cards. Let students ask question about that which they are uncertain. The teacher should try to anticipate those terms with which the students are unacquainted.

Also, the teacher should note that answers are provided for activities, which can be used at his or her discretion. Note the answer sheets are sometimes featured on the same page as student charts and will need to be cut apart.

The teacher may find it necessary to give aid initially to launch the students in a direction toward problem solving. It is essential that the students understand just what it is that they are to do for this activity in the task. The teacher may suggest that the first step in the problem solving process is to identify that task, as noted in each activity in this book.

Teachers may add additional information to the charts, tables, and maps that have been provided. Teachers may include additional clues on the cards if they feel it is necessary for the students to complete the activity.

Some of the problems contained in the activities would best be solved by using a computer and a spreadsheet program. It is assumed that students in the upper grades have access to computers and would already possess the skills necessary to utilize a spreadsheet program.

When using a spreadsheet program, the students will have to visualize just what information is needed and just what calculations will have to be computed. They may have to use trial and error to build a program and make changes or additions as they see the need.

The Jigsaw Technique

A helpful practice before some activities, especially those with clue cards with a lot of information on them, is to use a technique called the jigsaw. In the jigsaw, all team members who are identified as "A's" gather to review the information found on the "A" card. At the same time the B's, C's, and D's are doing the same thing with their respective clue cards. The students then reconvene their groups and begin working on the problem, with each member feeling somewhat knowledgeable about his or her information.

Using the Metacognitive Discussion

Included with each activity in this book is a Metacognitive Discussion feature that includes some suggested questions to start students reflecting on and talking about the learning process of a given activity. A debriefing or closure for an activity is essential. Give students the opportunity to talk about the process and how they worked through the problem.

Encourage each group to talk about how they worked at the problem. Let other students offer advice to those students who did not solve the problem and fully complete the task. Students may be prompted to write about the activity and the process they went through.

In Closing

This book is an attempt to make your social studies curriculum come alive. Our cooperative problem solving activities are simulations that provide for experiential learning, not simply the absorption of data. Sufficient information is provided on topics to enable the students to function as a problem-solving unit. Our simulations are interactive events. The activities allow for learning by discovery.

Constructivist teaching centers on the idea that students learn best when they construct their knowledge rather than reproduce someone else's knowledge. As scientist and philosopher Blaise Pascal stated, "We are usually convinced more easily by reasons we have found ourselves than by those which have occurred to others." This book is full of convergent, authentic, interesting, and holistic activities that extend and refine students' understanding of key ideas in social studies.

Using the approach in *Catch Them Thinking in Social Studies*, students have opportunities for active experimentation in solving problems that require the integration of knowledge, skills, and personal values. Our activities cross the varied content areas of social science and are often interdisciplinary in nature. They attempt to teach persistence, creativity, and the benefits of shared responsibility. Students learn that individual work effectiveness and team success are interrelated—a concept critical to students being competitive in today's workplace. Studies such as America 2000 illustrates that we need a work force that is not only proficient in basic skills but also can think, apply knowledge, and solve problems. As educators ready students for the world outside their classroom walls, there must be special emphasis placed on providing opportunities that develop skills necessary for success. It is our belief that the cooperative problem solving activities in this book are excellent sources of this type of opportunity.

This book was created with the classroom teacher in mind, to fill a void for ready-made activities for the social studies teacher to interject into their instruction. This strategy, field-tested in our classrooms, works.

Mickey Hickman

Erin O'Donnell Wiggington

References

Erickson, Tim. *United we solve*: *Math problems for groups*. Oakland, CA: eeps media.

DiBasso, Thomas V., Lorna C. Mason, and Christian G. Appy. 1991. *History of the United States*. Atlanta, GA: Houghton Mifflin Company.

Hoffman, Mark S., Ed. 1993. *The world almanac and book of facts*. New York, NY: Pharas Books, a Scripps Howard Company.

McClenaghan, William A. 1992. *Magruder's American government*. Needham, MS: Prentice Hall.

Sager, Robert J., and David M. Helgren. 1997. *World geography today*. Austin, TX: Holt, Rinehart and Winston.

Teacher's Reflection Page

For each cooperative problem-solving activity your students do, answer the following questions:

Generally, how did the activity go for the majority of the students?

_____

_____

_____

_____

What stumbling blocks did the students have to overcome?

_____

_____

_____

_____

What hints or assistance did you have to provide?

_____

_____

_____

_____

What adjustments do you want to make before you use this activity again?

_____

_____

_____

_____

What, if any, preparatory steps do you want to take before you assign the class another cooperative problem-solving activity?

_____

_____

_____

_____

Other comments:

_____

_____

_____

_____

PART I

Geography

Time Zones, Maps, and Population Counts

Geography:

Times Zones, Maps, and Population Counts

This part of *Catch Them Thinking in Social Studies* is designed for geography and math classrooms as well as for some history classrooms. The activities require students to take time and take care as they work with measurements, formulas, and/or visual clues.

The first four activities center around the fictional International Basketball Association (IBA).

"Globe Trotting" familiarizes students with latitude and longitude and challenges them to discern the itineraries of five IBA representatives. Students deduce the sequence of the representatives' destinations (described only by latitude and longitude), plot the coordinates on a grid, and use a world map to name the cities at those coordinates.

In "Time Zones," students construct a calculator that determines the time of day in IBA cities around the world. Each team makes a calculator with two dissimilarly sized paper plates and a fastener. They draw marks 15 degrees apart to simulate the world's 24 time zones on both wheels. On the smaller wheel, guided by information in the clue cards, students correctly place names of IBA cities.

In "Playoff Schedule," students use these calculators (or other reference material on time zones) and follow the league's rules given in the clue cards to schedule the IBA semifinal games. In "Satellite TV," they use both the calculators and the playoff schedule to arrange a timetable for simultaneous broadcasts of the games to fans in different time zones.

Students use visual clues and logic to label seven outline maps for "Maps of the United States and Canada." As they follow the clue cards, they also acquire some information about the agriculture, population, waterways, and topography of North America.

In "Demographics," students graph data on their own and neighboring localities and states from information they gather from the U.S. Census Bureau's Internet site. The scope broadens in "U.S. Population Clock Projections," in which they make various projections of the U.S. population. From the clue cards, they deduce and apply the Census Bureau's formula and criteria for computing the U.S. birth rate, migrant rate, citizen reentry rate, death rate, and adjusted rate. Students may use a spreadsheet program or a calculator or do the calculations by hand.

Then, in "World Population Clock Projections," students again employ Census Bureau formulas, this time to demonstrate the rate of change in the world's population. They project backward to identify the year the world population reached 4 billion people, and forward to the years in which it will reach first 7 billion and then 10 billion people. Students can use a spreadsheet program or a calculator or do the calculations by hand.

SkyLight Training and Publishing Inc.

The IBA: Globe Trotting

Activity 1

Extra materials needed:
✓ World atlases
✓ Globe

Students identify world itineraries of five representatives of the fictional International Basketball Association (IBA) by adding and subtracting longitude and latitude coordinates that they order in the correct sequence. Only New York City, the single departure point for the five travelers, is named; from that point, students calculate 23 other locations by their relative longitude and latitude. Students then plot the coordinates on a grid and use a world map to name the cities at those coordinates. No two travelers visit the same city, and no traveler visits more than five cities after leaving New York City.

Background Information

Mapmakers use vertical lines called meridians of longitude and horizontal lines called parallels of latitude. Longitude runs north and south, and latitude runs east and west. By following these vertical and horizontal lines and determining where these lines intersect, one can find locations on a map.

Lines of longitude start at 0 degrees at the prime meridian (the first line of longitude) and run to 180 degrees (located in the middle of the Pacific Ocean). Meridians of longitude west of the prime meridian are labeled with a W and those east of the prime meridian are labeled with an E. Parallels of latitude range from 0 degrees at the equator to 90 degrees north (N) at the North Pole and 90 degrees south (S) at the South Pole.

Objective

Students gain a thorough understanding of latitude and longitude by deducing separate itineraries of five world travelers.

Task

Discover and describe five persons' different itineraries using a common departure point, latitude and longitude coordinates, a grid (see figure 1.1), and a world map.

Answers

The league representatives traveled to the following cities in the order given for each.

Linda traveled first to London, then to Madrid, Rome, Athens, and Moscow.

Kristin traveled first to New Delhi, then to Jerusalem, Cairo, and Johannesburg.

Korey traveled first to Tokyo, then to Beijing, Manila, Sydney, and Melbourne.

Leila traveled first to Paris, then to Brussels, Amsterdam, Copenhagen, and Berlin.

Conor traveled first to Havana, then to Rio de Janeiro, Buenos Aires, and Mexico City.

Metacognitive Discussion

How do you think the system of using imaginary lines for latitude and longitude came to be invented? How do latitude and longitude lines on a globe differ from those on a map? Which countries are big on a map but much smaller on a globe, and why is there a difference? If you were a captain of a ship, would using only latitude and longitude help you stay on course?

SkyLight Training and Publishing Inc.

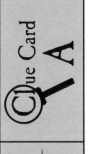

Clue Card A

1. Leila's fifth and final city is 13 degrees south of London and almost 24 degrees to the east.
2. By flying 22 degrees south and 18 degrees east, Korey arrived at his third city.
3. For her third stop, Kristin traveled 1 degree north and 4 degrees east.
4. Your job is to name the 23 cities and to list them according to which representative visited them and in the order he or she visited them.
5. Conor's first city was approximately 18 degrees east and 8 degrees south of Leila's first stop.
6. Kristin traveled 56 degrees north and 3 degrees east to arrive at her second stop.
7. Connect the points of each representative's travels. Personalize each rep's travels with a different color.

Clue Card B

1. Linda, Leila, Korey, Kristin, and Conor set out from New York City on Monday but headed out on different flights in different directions. New York City is located 40 degrees north by 74 degrees east.
2. The second city of Conor's itinerary was 4 degrees south and 6 degrees west of his first city.
3. From her first stop, Linda traveled 13 degrees south and 25 degrees west to get to her second destination.
4. Leila's first city was 75 degrees east and 11 degrees north of the city of her departure.
5. Kristin's second stop was 25 degrees south and 6 degrees west of Conor's final stop.

Clue Card C

1. Forty-two degrees east and 3 degrees south took Kristin to her final city.
2. Korey's first destination took him to 30 degrees south and 8 degrees east of his origination.
3. Leila's third city and fourth city are 1 degree apart in latitude, but the fourth city is 9 more degrees to the east.
4. Linda's final city was just a short stop from the fourth; a trip of only 4 degrees northward and 6 degrees to the east.
5. Linda's fourth stop took her 52 degrees to the south and 14 degrees to the east from the third city.
6. Traveling north 12 degrees and 15 degrees east to the coast, Korey reached his final stop.
7. A map or globe would be very useful.

Clue Card D

1. Kristin traveled 66 degrees south and 102 degrees east to reach her first assignment.
2. Linda's first stop could be located on a map at approximately 36 degrees north and 140 degrees east.
3. Destination three for Linda was a journey of 8 degrees to the south and 7 degrees to the east.
4. Conor's third stop was 3 degrees south and 1 degree east of his second city.
5. Korey traveled approximately 20 degrees south and about 10 degrees west to arrive at his second city.
6. Leila traveled 3 degrees south and 2 degrees east to get to her second city.
7. Plot their travels on the grid system provided.

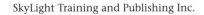

SkyLight Training and Publishing Inc.

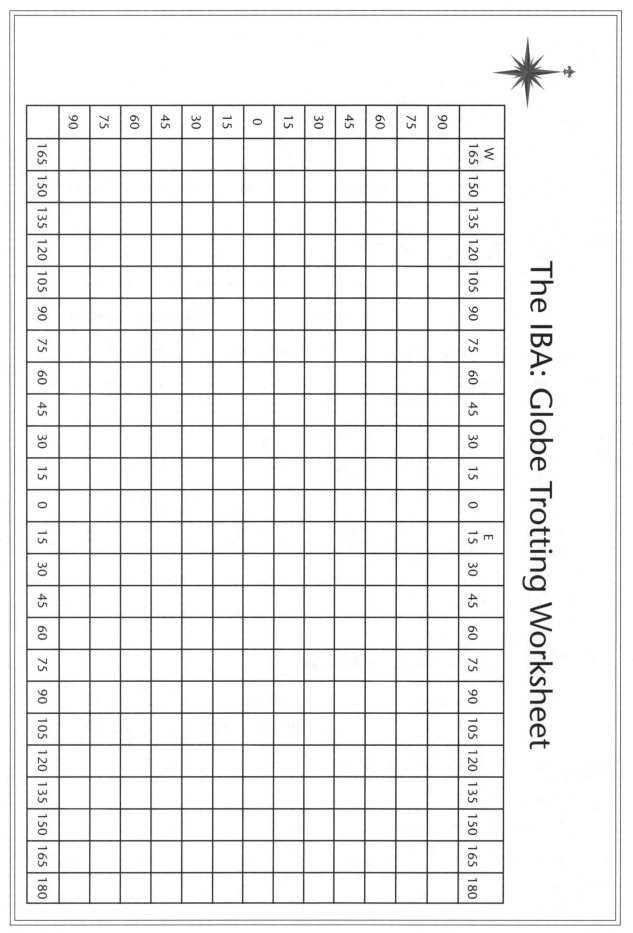

The IBA: Globe Trotting Worksheet

Figure 1.1

SkyLight Training and Publishing Inc.

The IBA: Time Zones

Activity 2

Students create a paper-plate calculator for telling time across the world. (They will use the calculator again in Activities 3 and 4.)

Background Information

Materials needed for each team are two paper plates of unequal size and one brass fastener so that students can make a mechanical time zone calculator. On the larger wheel, they mark off equal 15-degree sections to represent the 24 times zones, and label one line as 12:00 noon. On the smaller wheel, they draw one line and label it New York. After they fasten the plates together at their centers and align the marks of both wheels, students are ready to add cities' names in the correct time zones. A clue in the cards tells students to mark the cities moving eastward from New York City.

At the completion of the activity, students' calculators, when set at 12:00 noon for New York City, will reflect the following cities and times:

Answers: 12:00 Noon NY (Eastern Time)				
Berlin	6:00 P.M.	Moscow	8:00 P.M.
Paris	6:00 P.M.	Buenos Aires	7:00 P.M.
Brussels	6:00 P.M.	Jerusalem	7:00 P.M.
Rome	6:00 P.M.	Mexico City	11:00 A.M.
Melbourne	3:00 A.M.	Rio de Janeiro	2:00 P.M.
Manila	1:00 A.M.	New Delhi	10:30 P.M.
Tokyo	2:00 A.M.	Beijing	1:00 A.M.
Sydney	3:00 A.M.	London	5:00 P.M.

Objective

Students learn how the time zone system works and review locations of major world capitals.

Task

Students create a time calculator so they know what time it is in the cities where the fictional International Basketball Association has teams.

Metacognitive Discussion

How is the time zone system organized? How would you keep track of time if you were at the North Pole?

1. A circle has 360 degrees.
2. The teams—the Berlin Wall, the Brussels Sprouts, the Amsterdam Masters, the Paris Bourbons, and the Copenhagen Norse—do not have to worry about time zone travel when they play one another because they share the same time zone.
3. Ania, a fan of the IBA, departs Kennedy Airport in New York at 2:00 P.M. She will arrive at Heathrow Airport in London at 11:00 P.M.
4. A 7:00 P.M. game between the visiting Mexico City Amigos and the Rio de Janeiro Amazons can be viewed back in Mexico City at 3:00 P.M.
5. A feature of Argentina is large cattle ranches worked by Argentine cowboys, called "gauchos."

1. The Manila Ice travel one time zone to play the Samurai from Tokyo, and the Samurai travel one time zone to play the Sydney Roos.
2. Your task is to construct a calculator to determine time in the IBA cities.
3. The Johannesburg Diamonds and the Jerusalem Crusaders share the same time zone, and they are between the Bourbons' time zone and the Cossacks' time zone.
4. Please mark New York City on the smaller wheel first.
5. The Cobras are exactly halfway across their time zone so they play on the half hour, that is when it is "on the hour" for the rest of the league, it is half past the hour for New Delhi.

1. A typical flight from London to New York, or vice versa, takes four hours.
2. Ania's two-hour flight to Moscow departs London at 2:00 P.M. She anticipates it will take one hour to travel from the Moscow airport to the arena to watch an 8:00 P.M. game between the Cossacks and the London Bobbies.
3. The Boxers travel one time zone to play the Samurai, while the Samurai must travel 2 time zones to play the Roos.
4. There are 24 equidistant time zones.
5. Australia features two teams in this league, the Roos and the Mates that share the same time zone.
6. The team from Copenhagen (the Norse) share the same time zone as the Cardinals (the Italian entry).

1. To reach the Cobras' country, the Beijing Boxers travel west 2.5 time zones, and the Cossacks travel east 2.5 time zones.
2. Using New York City as the reference point, mark the other cities of the league at their appropriate places on the wheel.
3. Place the teams on the calculator moving eastward from New York City.
4. The Cobras' city is exactly halfway between Moscow and Beijing.
5. Melbourne and Sydney are two cities found in Australia.
6. The Amazon and the Cowboys share the time zone that is two hours ahead of U.S. Eastern Time.

The IBA: Playoff Schedule

Activity 3

Students work with time zone differences and the regulations of the fictional International Basketball Association to create an 18-day playoff schedule of at least 24 games. Students use the time zone calculators they assembled in Activity 2 or, an alternative, consult reference material or the Web site http://www.GMT2000.com/ for time zone information.

Background Information

When the sun is directly overhead a portion the earth, it is 12:00 noon in that time zone. Because the earth is rotating on its axis, noon occurs at different times in different locations. The earth makes one full rotation on its axis in a 24-hour time period, so it makes 1/24th of a complete rotation in one hour. There are 360 degrees in a circle (rotation), so the earth travels 15 degrees in each of those 24 hours. With every 15 degrees of earth rotation, a different location on earth experiences noon, or midnight, or any other hour of the day.

An imaginary line called the prime meridian passes through Greenwich, England. Through international agreement, the prime meridian is used as the starting point for calculating the time of day, called Greenwich Mean Time (GMT). For each 15 degrees east of the prime meridian, it is one hour of clock time later than Greenwich Mean Time. Each 15 degrees west of the prime meridian is an hour earlier than GMT. When it is 12:00 noon GMT, it is 1:00 P.M. in Copenhagen, Denmark, which is one hour east of the prime meridian. It is also 11:00 A.M. in the time zone one hour, or 15 degrees, to the west of the prime meridian.

SkyLight Training and Publishing Inc.

On the other side of the earth, directly opposite the prime meridian, is another important imaginary line of longitude, the International Date Line, located at 180 degrees longitude. If a person crosses this line traveling from the west to the east, that person gains a day. However, if one travels from east to west, one would lose a day.

Objective

Students learn of and follow multiple criteria to schedule a series of events for the teams or "seeds."

Task

Students create an 18-day schedule of 24 events according to rules and conditions found in the clue cards. They plan correct spacing of events and ensure that all events occur at a time of day appropriate in varying time zones.

Metacognitive Discussion

How do you organize a project with multiple objectives? Why is it time-consuming? How will you prepare the next time you have a project with multiple objectives?

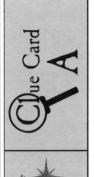

Clue Card A

1. The Johannesburg Diamonds are one of four teams to make the IBA playoffs. Their record is 54–26. They are the first seed.
2. Teams cannot have back-to-back game dates.
3. Teams must be given 48 hours to travel.
4. The highest seed is paired to play the lowest seed.
5. A total of 18 days is allotted to conduct and conclude both of the 7-game series.
6. The Melbourne Mates' record is 47 wins and 33 losses. They are the fourth seed.

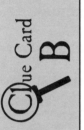

Clue Card B

1. The higher seed gets to open the series at home.
2. Consideration must be given to the visitors and the broadcast times back home ("redeye games").
3. The Buenos Aires Cowboys have a 51-29 record.
4. The Cobras from New Delhi finished the season with a 49-31 record.
5. The playoff series is to be played in the following fashion: 2-2-1-1-1. The higher seed plays two games at home, then two games away in a lower seed's arena, then one game at home, then one game away in a lower seed's arena, and finally one game at home if necessary.
6. Each team's opening home stand consists of two consecutive games at home before traveling. Then the teams must travel in the 2-2-1-1-1. The higher seed gets to play at home first.

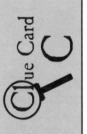

Clue Card C

1. Redeye times are at 2:00 A.M., 3:00 A.M., or 4:00 A.M.
2. There can never be more than one day that a game is not being played in either of the two semifinal series.
3. Your task is to come up with a playoff schedule for the two semifinal series.
4. Home games can never start before 12:00 noon or later than 9:30 P.M. (in the host's time zone).
5. The final three games are rotated on a home-home-home basis as needed.
6. The higher seed will play one more home game than the lower seed if seven games are needed.

Clue Card D

1. The playoffs may begin on May 2.
2. The second seed is paired to play the third seed.
3. Games from the two semifinals are not to be played on the same day/date.
4. Seeding is determined by win-loss records.
5. Please list the playoff schedule and the dates and times that they are to be played in the host city.
6. Please also include the broadcast times for the visiting city.

IBA Playoff Schedule Worksheet

Date MAY	Host Time	Visitor Time	Game #	Series – – –	Host City	GAME – – – – –

IBA Playoff Schedule Answers

Date MAY	Host Time	Visitor Time	Game #	Series – – –	Host City	GAME – – – – –
2	1:00 P.M.	9:00 P.M.	1	A (1 v 4)	JB	JB v MB
3	8:30 P.M.	12:00 P.M.	1	B (2 v 3)	ND	ND v BA
4	3:00 P.M.	9:00 P.M.	2	A	JB	JB v MB
5	7:30 P.M.	11:00 A.M.	2	B	ND	ND v BA
6	OPEN	OPEN	– –	– –	– –	TRAVEL
7	5:00 P.M.	9:00 A.M.	3	A	MB	MB v JB
8	1:00 P.M.	9:30 P.M.	3	B	BA	BA v ND
9	8:00 P.M.	12:00 P.M.	4	A	MB	MB v JB
10	3:00 P.M.	11:30 A.M.	4	B	BA	BA v ND
11	OPEN	OPEN	– –	– –	– –	TRAVEL
12	12:00 P.M.	8:00 P.M.	5	A	JB	JB v MB
13	4:30 P.M.	8:00 A.M.	5	B	ND	ND v BA
14	OPEN	OPEN	– –	– –	– –	TRAVEL
15	8:00 P.M.	12:00 P.M.	6	A	MB	JB v MB
16	4:30 P.M.	1:00 P.M.	6	B	BA	BA v ND
17	OPEN	OPEN	– –	– –	– –	TRAVEL
18	9:30 P.M.	5:30 A.M.	7	A	JB	JB v MB
19	6:00 P.M.	9:30 A.M.	7	B	ND	ND v BA

Legend:

JB is Johannesburg Diamonds.

MB is Melbourne Mates.

ND is New Delhi Cobras.

BA is Buenos Aires Cowboys.

Figure 1.3

SkyLight Training and Publishing Inc.

The IBA: Satellite TV

Activity 4

Students now employ both the time calculator they created in Activity 2 and the playoff schedule they created in Activity 3 to schedule simultaneous broadcasts of those games across time zones. As an alternative to Activities 2 and/or 3, the teacher can direct the students to the following Web site for a time calculator: http://www.GMT2000.com/ and/or supply students with the playoff schedule (see Activity 3, figure 1.3). The best site for this option is www.worldtimezone.com/.

Background Information

Your team works for the network that is broadcasting the International Basketball Association (IBA) playoff games. Your job is to prepare the broadcast schedule so fans around the world can watch the playoffs as the games are being played.

Objective

Students organize a schedule of multiple events by time zones for simultaneous broadcasting.

Task

Create a television broadcast schedule using a time calculator, game schedule, and criteria presented in the clue cards.

Metacognitive Discussion

How do you organize a project with multiple objectives? Why is it time-consuming? How will you prepare the next time you have a problem with multiple objectives? How does ensuring that the same thing occurs simultaneously at different places differ from other kinds of projects?

1. Arrange the schedule so that fans in Denver, Colorado, may watch the games.
2. Arrange the schedule so the fans in Athens, Greece, may watch the games.
3. You may want to consult the IBA's playoff schedule.

1. Arrange the schedule so that fans in Los Angeles, California, may watch the games.
2. Arrange the schedule so the fans in Tokyo, Japan, may watch the games.
3. Arrange the schedule so the fans in Moscow, Russia, may watch the games.

1. Arrange the schedule so the fans in New Orleans, Louisiana, may watch the games.
2. Arrange the schedule so the fans in Rome, Italy, may watch the games.
3. You may want to consult the IBA's playoff schedule.

1. Arrange the schedule so the fans in London, England, may watch the games.
2. Arrange the schedule so the fans in Boston, Massachusetts, may watch the games.
3. Arrange the schedule so the fans in Sydney, Australia, may watch the games.

The IBA: Satellite TV Worksheet

Date May	2	3	4	5	6	7	8	9	10	11	12	13	14	15	16	17	18	19
Los Angeles																		
Denver																		
New Orleans																		
Boston																		
Athens																		
Tokyo																		
Moscow																		
Rome																		
London																		
Sydney																		

Figure 1.4

SkyLight Training and Publishing Inc.

The IBA: Satellite TV Answers

Date May	2	3	4	5	6	7	8	9	10	11	12	13	14	15	16	17	18	19
Los Angeles	10 A.M.	7 A.M.	12 P.M.	4:30 P.M.		11 P.M.	10 A.M.	2 A.M.	12 P.M.		9 A.M.	3 A.M.		2 A.M.	1:30 P.M.		10:30 A.M.	3 P.M.
Denver	11 A.M.	8 A.M.	1 P.M.	5:30 P.M.		12 A.M.	11 A.M.	3 A.M.	1 P.M.		10 A.M.	4 A.M.		3 A.M.	2:30 P.M.		11:30 A.M.	4 P.M.
New Orleans	12 P.M.	9 A.M.	2 P.M.	6:30 P.M.		1 A.M.	12 P.M.	4 A.M.	2 P.M.		11 A.M.	5 A.M.		4 A.M.	3:30 P.M.		12:30 P.M.	5 P.M.
Boston	1 P.M.	10 A.M.	3 P.M.	7:30 P.M.		2 A.M.	1 P.M.	5 A.M.	3 P.M.		12 P.M.	6 A.M.		5 A.M.	4:30 P.M.		1:30 P.M.	6 P.M.
Athens	8 P.M.	5 P.M.	11 P.M.	2:30 A.M.		9 A.M.	8 P.M.	12 P.M.	10 P.M.		7 P.M.	1 P.M.		12 P.M.	11:30 P.M.		8:30 P.M.	1 A.M.
Tokyo	5 A.M.	12 A.M.	7 A.M.	9:30 A.M.		4 P.M.	3 A.M.	7 P.M.	5 A.M.		4 A.M.	8 P.M.		7 P.M.	6:30 A.M.		11:30 A.M.	8 A.M.
Moscow	9 P.M.	6 P.M.	11 P.M.	3:30 A.M.		10 A.M.	9 P.M.	11 A.M.	11 P.M.		8 P.M.	2 P.M.		1 P.M.	12:30 A.M.		5:30 A.M.	2 A.M.
Rome	7 P.M.	4 P.M.	10 P.M.	1:30 A.M.		8 A.M.	7 P.M.	10 A.M.	9 P.M.		6 P.M.	12 P.M.		11 A.M.	10:30 P.M.		3:30 A.M.	12 A.M.
London	6 P.M.	3 P.M.	8 P.M.	12:30 A.M.		7 A.M.	6 P.M.	10 A.M.	8 P.M.		5 P.M.	11 A.M.		10 A.M.	9:30 P.M.		2:30 A.M.	11 P.M.
Sydney	4 A.M.	1 A.M.	6 A.M.	12:30 A.M.		5 P.M.	4 A.M.	8 P.M.	6 A.M.		3 A.M.	9 P.M.		8 P.M.	7:30 A.M.		12:30 P.M.	9 A.M.

Maps of the United States and Canada

Activity 5

Students label seven maps by using clues and deduction to identify the states in areas (Pacific West, Interior West, Midwest, New England, Mid-Atlantic, South) of the United States as well as the provinces and territories of Canada.

Objective

Students correctly label maps of different areas of North America.

Task

Students use the clues to identify the states, provinces, or territories on seven maps of the United States and Canada.

Metacognitive Discussion

Which states, provinces, or areas did you find difficult to identify, and why? What was the last state, province, or area you identified, and why was it the last one? What can you do next time to more quickly identify areas on a map? How do you suppose the different boundaries were set?

SkyLight Training and Publishing Inc.

Teacher Note

Below are the titles of the seven regions of North America, each with a listing of the states (provinces and territories in Canada) that students will locate on the following seven maps. Included are clues listed in a sequence helpful for labeling the individual maps; however, sometimes students will use logic and elimination to complete a map.

Pacific West

Alaska, California, Hawaii, Oregon, Washington

The following clues help to indicate state locations: D1, C4 and B1, D3, C3, A2, B4

Interior West

Arizona, Colorado, Idaho, Kansas, Montana, Nebraska, Nevada, New Mexico, North Dakota, Oklahoma, South Dakota, Utah, Wyoming

The following clues help to indicate state locations: A1, A4, B3, C4, D1, D4, B1, C2, D3

Midwest

Illinois, Indiana, Iowa, Michigan, Missouri, Minnesota, Ohio, Wisconsin

The following clues help to indicate state locations: A1, D4, D2, D3, C1, C3, A2, A3, B3.

New England

Connecticut, Maine, Massachusetts, New Hampshire, Rhode Island, Vermont

The following clues help to indicate state locations: A1, B1, C1, D1, C3

Mid-Atlantic

Delaware, Maryland, New Jersey, New York, Pennsylvania, West Virginia

The following clues help to indicate state locations: C1, B1, A1, C4, D1, C2

South

Alabama, Arkansas, Florida, Georgia, Kentucky, Louisiana, Mississippi, North Carolina, South Carolina, Tennessee, Texas, Virginia

The following clues help to indicate state locations: A3, B1, B2, B3, C1, A1, D3, A2

Canada

Provinces: Alberta, British Columbia, Manitoba, New Brunswick, Newfoundland, Nova Scotia, Ontario, Prince Edward Island, Quebec, Saskatchewan

Territories: Northwest, Nunavut, Yukon

The following clues help to indicate province and territory locations: D5, A1, B1, C5, B1, A4 , C5, A5, C1, D6, D6, B1, D3, B1, B1, D4, D1, B4, A5

1. More than 90 percent of California's 31 million people live in urban areas.
2. Alaska's closest neighboring state is Washington.
3. Some of America's hottest temperatures and scarcest rainfall annually can be found in California's Death Valley.
4. Seattle and Tacoma are two Washington cities found in the Puget Sound area.

1. The United States's first-rated and third-rated states in land area comprise the Pacific West.
2. The Sierra Nevada are mountains located in California.
3. The deepest lake in the United States is Crater Lake, which is found in Oregon.
4. The Pacific Northwest states of Oregon and Washington receive a great amount of rainfall annually.

1. South of San Francisco is land rich in silicon, the material used in computer chips; hence the name "Silicon Valley."
2. The San Andreas Fault is located in California.
3. The Cascades are a volcanic mountain range running southward through three states from Washington to northern California.
4. Texas ranks ahead of California in land area, but behind California in population.

1. Hawaii will not have a border dispute with anyone.
2. Mount St. Helens is an active volcano located in the state of Washington.
3. San Diego is California's third-largest urban area and is located near the border of Mexico.
4. Correctly identify on the outline map the states of the Pacific Northwest.

Pacific West

SkyLight Training and Publishing Inc.

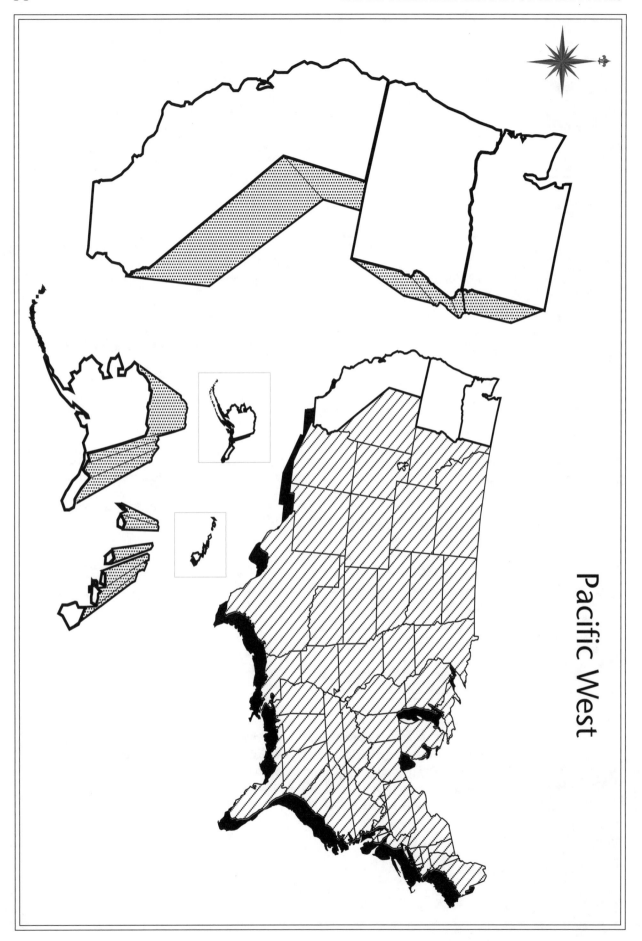

Pacific West

Figure 1.6

SkyLight Training and Publishing Inc.

1. Colorado is bordered by seven Interior West states, including its neighbor, Wyoming, which is bordered by six states.
2. Tourism is big business in the Interior West, with national parks, ski resorts, and game fishing and game hunting among the attractions that draw tourists.
3. The Rocky Mountains are a part of the Interior West and are located in six of the region's thirteen states.
4. A traveler from Canada would have to travel due south through four Interior West states to reach Oklahoma.

1. The states of Arizona, Montana, North Dakota, New Mexico, and Idaho all need "border patrols."
2. The Grand Canyon is found in Arizona.
3. Utah can be considered a western neighbor of both Colorado and Wyoming.
4. Texas, although a part of the South, joins the Dakotas and five other western states to form the "Wheat Belt."

1. Mining has been an important industry of the Interior West.
2. Citizens of New Mexico have to travel due north in order to take the most direct route to Montana.
3. The Rocky Mountains are younger than the Eastern mountains (Appalachians).
4. Of all the states in the Interior West, the state with the westernmost longitude is Nevada.

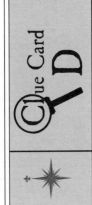

1. Only one state lies between Arizona and the Pacific Ocean.
2. The Great Plains are a part of the physical geography of the Interior West.
3. Nebraska lies south of North Dakota and immediately due north of Kansas.
4. Idaho shares a border with northeastern Nevada.
5. Correctly identify on the outline map the states of the Interior West.

Interior West

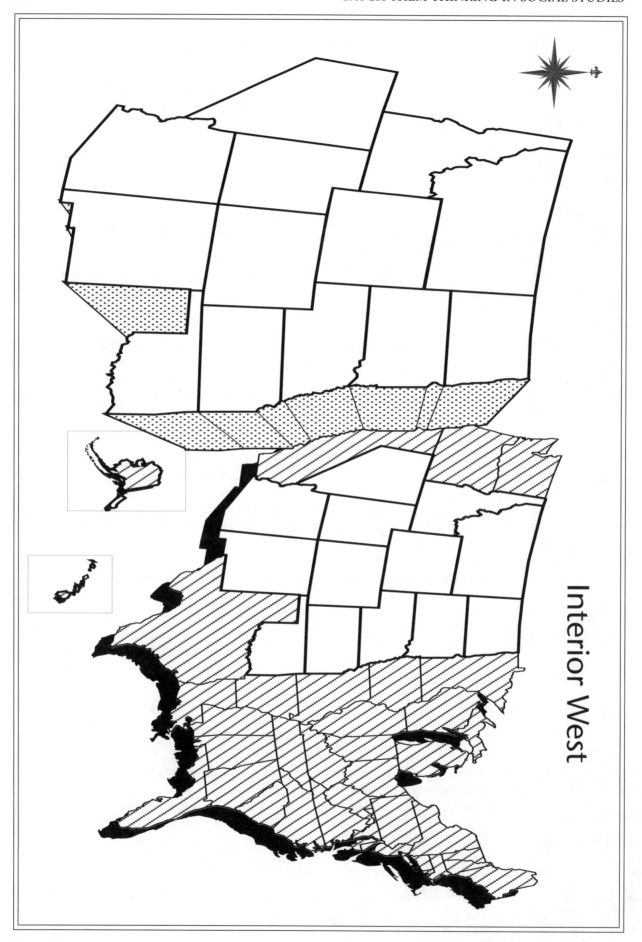

Interior West

Figure 1.7

SkyLight Training and Publishing Inc.

1. Michigan has a peninsula bordered by four of the five Great Lakes.
2. Detroit, Michigan; Chicago, Illinois; and Cleveland, Ohio, are three great cities of the Midwest.
3. The northernmost states of the Midwest, Minnesota, Michigan, and Wisconsin, are collectively known as the "Dairy Belt."
4. Great rivers such as the Mississippi, Missouri, and Ohio flow through the Midwestern states.

1. Wisconsin, Minnesota, Illinois, Indiana, and Ohio all have shoreline along the Great Lakes.
2. The Great Lakes contain about 20 percent of the world's fresh surface water.
3. If one travels due north from Des Moines, the capital of Iowa, one only has to travel through the state of Minnesota to reach the Canadian border.
4. Corn is grown in all of the Midwestern states; a lot of it is used to feed livestock.

1. Michigan's southern neighbors are Indiana and Ohio.
2. Most of the land in the Midwest is flat and level.
3. Cleveland and Chicago both have shoreline on a Great Lake, but to leave one city to travel by land to the other city, one has to travel through another state.
4. St. Louis, Missouri, and the Twin Cities in Minnesota are also large important Midwestern cities.

1. More than 30 million people live in the three Midwestern states of Illinois, Michigan, and Ohio.
2. Missouri is a landlocked state bordered by eight other states, including its northern neighbor, Iowa.
3. Illinois's western border shares state lines with both Missouri and Iowa.
4. The state of Michigan's land form is divided into two separate land masses by two Great Lakes.
5. Correctly identify on the outline map the states of the Midwest.

Midwest

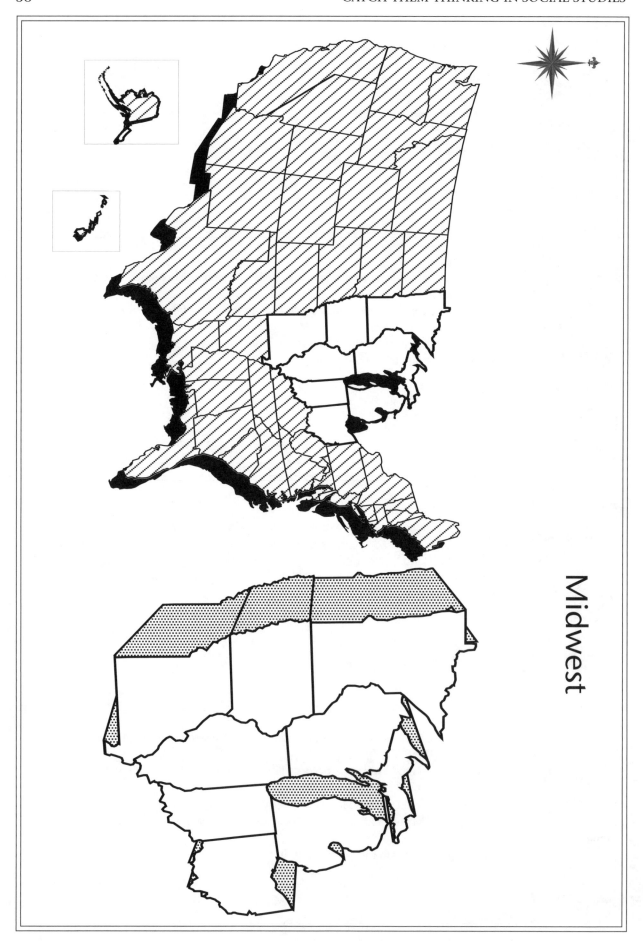

Midwest

Figure 1.6   SkyLight Training and Publishing Inc.

1. One could drive across the state length or width of Rhode Island more quickly than that of any other New England state.
2. Long Island Sound is off the coast of Connecticut.
3. The Connecticut River travels through four of the New England states.
4. Correctly identify the states of New England on the outline map.

1. Massachusetts is the only state to be bordered by four other New England states.
2. The Connecticut River serves as the western border to the state that serves as Maine's southwestern border.
3. The Green Mountains are located in Vermont, while the White Mountains are found in New Hampshire.
4. Correctly identify the states of New England on the outline map.

1. Settlers leaving Massachusetts for religious freedom had to travel south to found the community that became the Connecticut colony.
2. Penobscot Bay is off the coast of Maine.
3. Vermont lies further west than does New Hampshire.
4. Correctly identify the states of New England on the outline map.

New England

1. Vermont is the only New England state that does not have an Atlantic Ocean coastline.
2. Maine is bordered by only one other New England state.
3. Nantucket Sound is off the coast of Massachusetts.
4. Correctly identify the states of New England on the outline map.

SkyLight Training and Publishing Inc.

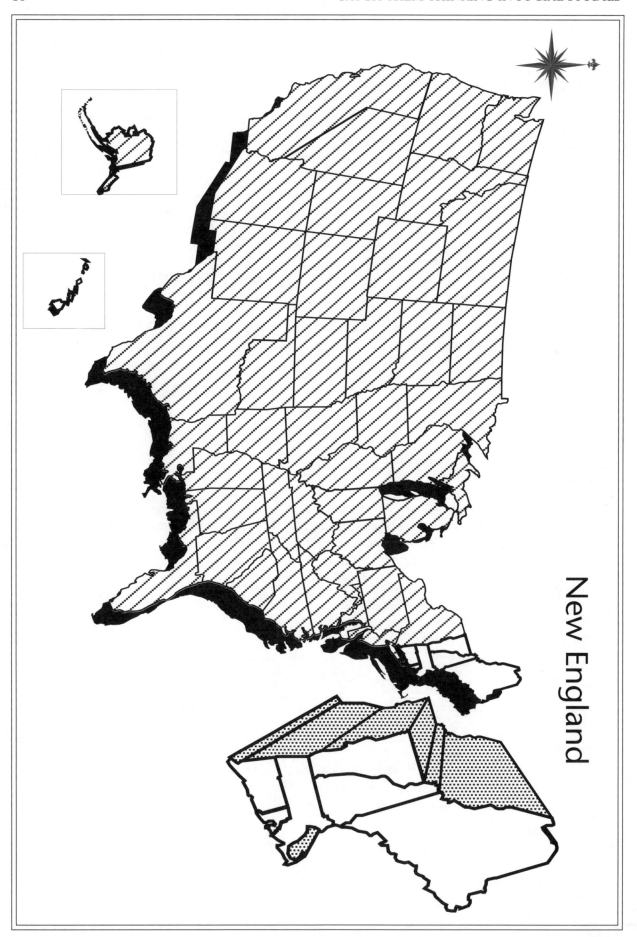

New England

Figure 1.9

SkyLight Training and Publishing Inc.

1. Pennsylvania has Mid-Atlantic neighbors to the north and the south.
2. The Appalachian Mountains run through the Mid-Atlantic states.
3. Pittsburgh, Pennsylvania, is the region's largest industrial city.
4. Canada borders the northernmost Mid-Atlantic state.

1. West Virginia and Pennsylvania are two Mid-Atlantic states that do not have a coastline.
2. Three rivers converge on Pittsburgh, which has the nation's largest inland harbor.
3. New York state's population ranks second in the United States behind that of California.

1. New York boasts a great tourist attraction, the Niagara Falls, which it shares with Canada. In Canada, these falls are known as the Horseshoe Falls.
2. The fictional Mason-Dixon line separating the North from the South lies in the state of Maryland.
3. West Virginia has supplied the nation with bituminous coal for decades.
4. New Jersey separates New York and Delaware.

1. New Jersey is bordered by three states, one of which is landlocked.
2. Crabs, oysters, and lobsters are fished from Maryland's Chesapeake Bay.
3. New York City is the largest city in both the Mid-Atlantic region and the nation.
4. Correctly identify the Mid-Atlantic states on the outline map.

Mid-Atlantic

SkyLight Training and Publishing Inc.

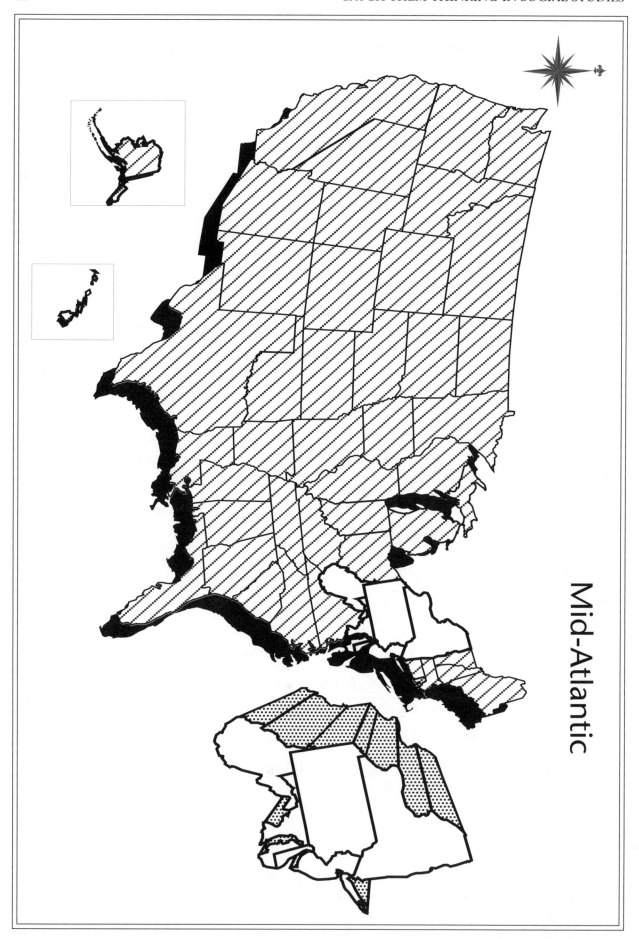

Mid-Atlantic

Figure 1.10

SkyLight Training and Publishing Inc.

1. Richmond, Virginia, served as the capital of the Confederacy, and it was located in the northernmost Southern state.
2. South Carolina lies between Georgia (to its south) and, naturally, this state.
3. Texas is the westernmost state in the region.

1. Louisiana and Arkansas border Texas.
2. Arkansas is a landlocked state.
3. Tennessee is the only other Southern landlocked state.
4. Tennessee borders five other Southern states.

1. One Southern state, Florida, is a peninsula. It is bordered by water on three sides.
2. Montgomery was the first capital of the Confederacy, and it also serves as the capital of the state between Mississippi and Georgia.
3. Kentucky is bordered by Tennessee and Virginia.
4. Correctly identify the states of the South on the outline map.

1. Nine Southern states have coasts with saltwater.
2. Five Southern states border the Gulf of Mexico, and the waters of the Atlantic Ocean also touch five states.
3. Alabama has shoreline on the Gulf of Mexico, but Georgia does not.

South

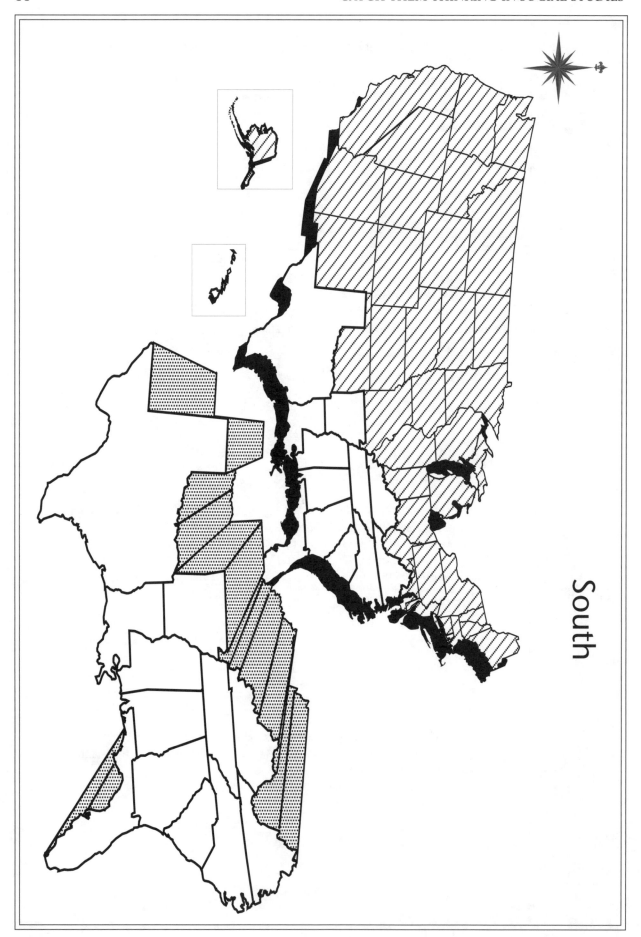

South

Figure 1.11   SkyLight Training and Publishing Inc.

Clue Card A

1. Saskatchewan is bordered by two provinces, and the Northwest Territory is its neighbor to the north.
2. In 1713, the British deported the French who were living in Nova Scotia to the then-French-owned Louisiana.
3. Canada is the world's second-largest country in land area.
4. The Canadian North consists of the three territories: the Yukon, the Northwest, and the Nunavut. All 10 provinces are located south of the territories.
5. Saskatchewan is bordered by two provinces, but British Columbia is not one of them.
6. The island province of Nova Scotia is about three times the size of its neighboring province, Prince Edward Island.

Clue Card B

1. The Nunavut territory, Quebec, Ontario, and Saskatchewan's neighboring province all have shoreline on the Hudson Bay.
2. Canada's current population is approximately 27 million people.
3. The Yukon Territory has Alaska as its neighbor.
4. The British North America Act of 1867 created the Dominion of Canada, which joined together the neighboring provinces of Ontario, Quebec, New Brunswick, and Nova Scotia to be governed by a parliament and a prime minister.
5. The Nunavut and the Northwest Territory do not share a border with the United States.

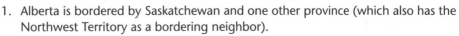

Clue Card C

1. Alberta is bordered by Saskatchewan and one other province (which also has the Northwest Territory as a bordering neighbor).
2. Winnipeg, a city located in Manitoba, serves as the nation's collection and shipping center.
3. Fishing is an important industry for both Prince Edward Island and British Columbia.
4. Toronto is the provincial capital of Ontario.
5. The Nunavut is a broken land mass consisting of several islands.
6. British Columbia is the only province that has two of the Canadian territories on its border.

Canada

Clue Card D

1. New Brunswick lies between two provinces and shares a short border with the state of Maine in the northeastern United States.
2. One of Canada's most important exports is its wheat crop.
3. Newfoundland does not share a border with the United States.
4. Quebec is bordered by three other Canadian provinces.
5. The Northwest Territory is Canada's largest landmass.
6. The most direct route for citizens of Winnipeg to reach British Columbia is to travel through Saskatchewan.

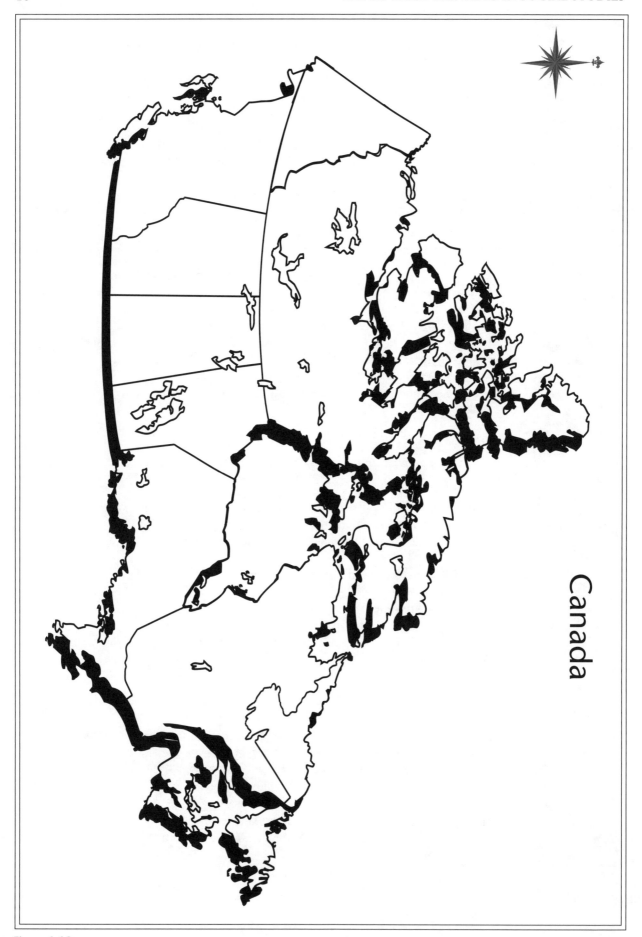

Canada

Figure 1.12

SkyLight Training and Publishing Inc.

Demographics

Activity 6

<table>
<tr>
<td>
Extra materials needed:
✓ Graph paper
✓ Scissors
✓ Tape
</td>
<td>
Students use Internet sites www.census.gov/population/ and http://govinfo.kerr.orst.edu/stateis.html to acquire demographic information on their own and neighboring localities and states. They will use graph paper to construct eight graphs of the data. Students will need previous experience in making pyramid, vertical bar, circle, and horizontal line graphs.
</td>
</tr>
</table>

Background Information

Demography is the science of human population, especially of human numbers and their changes over time. Birth and death rates, marital patterns, migration patterns, and population distributions are studied in demography. Demographics are used to ascertain trends and predict probabilities.

Objective

Students graph local demographic information gathered from their research on the Internet.

Task

Students will use local demographic data to construct two pyramid graphs, two vertical bar graphs, three circle graphs, and one horizontal line graph.

Metacognitive Discussion

How does working with graphs help you to better understand other graphs that you encounter in other readings? When else can you use graphs to help you understand or display percentages?

SkyLight Training and Publishing Inc.

Clue Card A

1. Construct a vertical bar graph based on the population of your state by the following age distributions: 1–18, 19–34, 35–49, 50–64, over 65.
2. A circle graph is also called a pie chart.
3. An Internet address essential to completing this activity is www.census.gov/population/
4. Construct a horizontal line graph that compares populations of ages 6 and under; 12–18; 25–29; 40–44; and 55–59 for the four neighboring localities.

Clue Card B

1. Create a circle graph showing the breakdown of ethnic groups in the four states that border your state or your state's closest neighbors: White, African American, Hispanic, Asian, Native American.
2. An Internet site crucial to completing this activity is http://govinfo.kerr.orst.edu/stateis.html.
3. Construct a pie chart showing the breakdown of ethnic groups (White, African American, Hispanic, Asian, Native American) in your chosen locality.
4. The site should give you first a United States map, then a state map, and, finally, a site with 1990 demographic information.

Clue Card C

1. Construct a vertical bar graph based on the population of your chosen locality by the following age distributions: 1–18, 19–34, 35–49, 50–64, Over 65.
2. Once you reach the site, select the state you live in.
3. Construct a pyramid graph. Compare your locality with one neighboring locality based on population by the following age distributions: 1–9, 10–19, 20–29, 30–39, 40–49, 50–59, and 60–69.

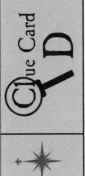

Clue Card D

1. Compare your locality with its four closest neighbors.
2. Once you find your state's map on the Web, select the locality in which you live.
3. Construct a circle graph depicting the total population of your locality's four closest neighbors.
4. Select one other state and construct a pyramid graph comparing it with your state by the age distribution data you find at your site (for example, 1–9, 10–19, 20–29, 30–39, 40–49, 50–59, and 60–69).

U.S. Population Clock Projections

Activity 7

Students make various projections of the U.S. population after they deduce and use the United States Census Bureau's formula and criteria for computing the U.S. birth rate, migrant rate, citizen reentry rate, death rate, and adjusted rate.

Background Information

Create the following time categories as rows: 1 minute, 1 hour, 1 day, 1 week, 1 month, and 1 year (all to be converted to seconds). As columns, use the following categories: seconds, birth rate, migrant rate, citizen reentry rate, death rate, and adjusted rate. Calendars for 1998 through 2010 may be needed for exact determination of years, days, and other variables, such as leap years.

Objective

Students deduce a statistical formula, apply it to very large numbers, and project how those numbers will change by specific dates in the future.

Task

Students make various projections of the U.S. population by using a spreadsheet program or a calculator or by doing the calculations by hand.

SkyLight Training and Publishing Inc.

Metacognitive Discussion

How did you find the answers? Why were some teams' projections different from other teams' projections? How do you make sure you are working accurately with very large numbers? How can you avoid making mistakes the next time you work with very large numbers?

U.S. Population Clock
Projections Worksheet

What will be the projected population of the United States for March 23, 1998 (2:00 P.M. EST)?	
What will be the projected population of the United States for January 1, 2010 (2:00 P.M. EST)?	
What was the projected population of the United States for March 23, 2003 (2:00 P.M. EST)?	
What was the projected population of the United States for February 23, 1998 (2:00 P.M. EST)?	
How often does the United States gain a person to its resident population?	
What will be the projected population of the United States for January 1, 2000 (2:00 P.M. EST)?	

Figure 1.13

	Seconds	Birth Rate	Death Rate	Migrant Rate	Reentry Rate	Adjusted Rate
1 minute						
1 hour						
1 day						
1 week						
1 month						
1 year						

Figure 1.14

U.S. Population Clock Projections
Worksheet Answers

What will be the projected population of the United States for March 23, 1998 (2:00 P.M. EST)?	269,257,132
What will be the projected population of the United States for January 1, 2010 (2:00 P.M. EST)?	294,474,703
What was the projected population of the United States for March 23, 2003 (2:00 P.M. EST)?	269,379,661
What was the projected population of the United States for February 23, 1998 (2:00 P.M. EST)?	271,347,413
How often does the United States gain a person to its resident population?	1 person every 15 seconds
What will be the projected population of the United States for January 1, 2000 (2:00 P.M. EST)?	273,163,463

Figure 1.15

	Seconds	Birth Rate	Death Rate	Migrant Rate	Reentry Rate	Adjusted Rate
1 minute	60	75	5	2	–	4
1 hour	3,600	450	300	92	–	242
1 day	86,400	10,800	7,200	2,215	19	5,835
1 week	604,800	75,600	50,400	15,508	135	40,843
1 month	2,592,000	324,000	215,000	66,462	579	175,041
1 year	31,557,600	3,944,700	2,629,800	809,169	7,055	2,131,124

Figure 1.16

SkyLight Training and Publishing Inc.

Clue Card A

1. In the United States, the death rate is 1.5 times the birth rate.
2. The U.S. resident population is defined as the number of persons who are living in the United States at any given moment.
3. Net migration is added to the resident population.
4. One hour equals 3,600 seconds.
5. What is the projected population of the United States for March 2, 2003, at 2:00 P.M. EST?

Clue Card B

1. What is the projected population of the United States on January 1, 2010, at 2:00 P.M. EST?
2. The resident population excludes overseas Armed Forces personnel and their dependents.
3. A U.S. citizen returns from abroad every 74 minutes and 33 seconds.
4. Deaths are subtracted from the resident population.
5. What was the population of the United States on March 23, 1998, at 2:00 P.M. EST?
6. The adjusted rate is the calculation that results from subtracting those categories that take away from the population (such as the death rate) from the total of the categories that add to the population.

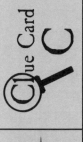

Clue Card C

1. The resident population is usually adjusted on a monthly basis.
2. In the United States, a birth occurs every 8 seconds.
3. Births are added to the resident population.
4. On February 23, 1999, at 2:00 P.M. EST, the resident population of the United States was 271,347,413.
5. What was the population of the United States one year later, on February 23, 1999, at 2:00 P.M. EST?
6. There are 75 persons born in the United States every 10 minutes.

Clue Card D

1. How often is a person added to the United States' resident population?
2. The resident population also excludes any U.S. citizens who are living outside the county.
3. The vital statistics that affect the resident population of the United States are births, deaths, and migration.
4. An international migrant enters the United States every 39 seconds.
5. The resident population includes the 50 states and the District of Columbia.
6. What is the projected population of the United States on January 1, 2000, at 2:00 P.M. EST?

Figure 1.12

SkyLight Training and Publishing Inc.

World Population Clock Projections

Activity 8

Students employ the statistical formulas used by the U.S. Census Bureau to demonstrate the rate of change in the world population, and they estimate the year the world population reached 4 billion people and the years in which it will reach 7 billion and 10 billion. Students can use a spreadsheet program or a calculator or do the calculations by hand.

Objective

Students apply statistical formulas to determine the rate of change (from by the second to by the year) in the world population and project the years in which the population increased or will increase to specific numbers.

Task

Students use formulas to complete a table of the rate of change in the world's population and project when the world population reached 4 billion people and in which years it will reach 7 billion and 10 billion people.

Metacognitive Discussion

How did you find the answers? Why were some teams' projections different from other teams' projections? How do you make sure you are working accurately when you are making projections? What will you remember to do the next time you make projections?

1. On February 23, 1998, the world's population was estimated at 5,898,633,000.
2. What is the world's projected population for January 1, 2000?
3. In a year's time, the world's population increases by 78,451,085.
4. The birth rate is referred to as the fertility rate.

1. Fill in the holes in the Start-Up table.
2. There are 227 countries in the world with a minimum population of 5,000.
3. In what year will the world's population reach 7 billion people?
4. Mortality rate refers to the death rate.

1. The world's birth rate is 252 births per minute.
2. The world's death rate is 1.7 deaths per second.
3. The world's population is affected by birth and death. In what year will the world's population reach 10 billion people?

1. On February 23, 1998, the world's population was estimated at 5,898,633,000.
2. How many deaths occur in a day's time?
3. Calculate the year in which the world's population reached the 4-billion mark.
4. How many deaths occur in a month's time?

World Population Projections
Start-UpTable

Time Units	Births	Deaths	Change
Year			78,451,085
Month			
Day		2400*1.7	
Hour		60*(60*1.7)	
Minute		252	
Second			1.7

Figure 1.17

Answers:

Time Units	Births	Deaths	Change
Year	130,636,800	52.876,800	78,451,085
Month	10,886,400	4,406,400	6,537,590
Day	362,880	146,880	217,920
Hour	15,120	6,120	1,197
Minute	252	102	19.95
Second	4.2	1.7	0.3325

Figure 1.18

World Population Clock Worksheet

What will be the world's projected population on January 1, 2000?	
Approximately in what year will the world's population reach 7 billion people?	
In what year will the world's population reach 10 billion people?	
How many deaths occur in a days time?	
Calculate in which year did the world's population reached the 4 billion mark?	
How many deaths occur in a month's time?	

Figure 1.19

Answers:

What will be the world's projected population on January 1, 2000?	6,044,865,000
Approximately in what year will the world's population reach 7 billion people?	2,012 (14 years)
In what year will the world's population reach 10 billion people?	2,051
How many deaths occur in a days time?	146,880
Calculate in which year did the world's population reached the 4 billion mark?	1,974
How many deaths occur in a month's time?	44,064,000

Figure 1.20

Figure 1.14

SkyLight Training and Publishing Inc.

PART II

Politics

U.S. Political Processes

Politics:

U.S. Political Processes

The activities in this part were created with the civics, government, or political science teacher in mind. The activities provide information and discussion materials for a wide range of political topics.

In the President's Cabinet, students are required to read the information and determine when the cabinet departments were created.

In the Apportionment activity, the methods to apportion or award seats in the United States House of Representatives are studied. There have been several different methods employed over the course of time. The students will complete the missing information for the chart that accompanies the activity.

In Apportionment: The Equal Proportions Method activity, the current method that is being used by the House of Representatives is explored. The rules and explanation of the Equal Proportions Methods is covered in the activity. A spreadsheet program is needed to generate the data needed to correctly answer the information called for on the chart.

In the fourth and fifth activities the students will look at the process of gerrymandering, drawing political districts with an end in mind. In Gerrymandering a State the students will actually draw districts on paper using the charts and the scenarios specified in the clues. In the Gerrymandering a County activity, the students are asked to design plans that gerrymander a county using the criteria spelled out in the clue cards.

In the Electoral College activity, students are asked to examine this institution and learn how it works and about the pros and cons of the system. Students will learn about the defects in the Electoral College system by looking at the Election of 1824. Students are asked to provide the information missing in the table provided with the activity.

The next activity takes a look at proposed legislation in the United States. "Capitol" Murder: How to Kill a Bill examines the different procedures that dispose of legislation. The student will be able to correctly fill in the missing information on the table that accompanies the activity.

In the Coming to America activity, the students are familiarized with immigration laws and regulations. In this activity the students will rank various characters in the order that they would be allowed to enter the United States.

SkyLight Training and Publishing Inc.

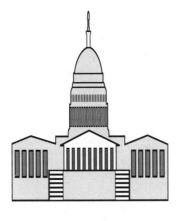

The President's Cabinet

Activity 9

Students gain perspective on the increasing complexity of both the nation and the president's duties as they trace the historical development of the president's cabinet.

Background Information

Students may need to understand the duties and responsibilities (or lack thereof) of an "advisor" before beginning this activity.

The president's cabinet is an informal advisory troupe whose members are chosen by the president. It is informal in the sense that the U.S. Constitution has no words dealing with it, nor has Congress officially created such a body.

George Washington had a four-member cabinet, and through usage and custom the cabinet has grown to 14 members, all of whom head executive departments. There are no qualifications for the position of cabinet member, except that the individual must be nominated by the president and approved by the Senate.

Objective

Students interpret sequence clues and learn 14 substantive areas that emerged in growing importance and differentiation to a U.S. president in governing the country.

Task

On the chart, students rank cabinet departments in the order they were created.

Input

State–1789, Treasury–1789, Interior–1849, Justice–1870, Agriculture–1889, Commerce–1903, Labor–1913, Defense–1949, Health and Human Services–1953, Housing and Urban Development–1965, Transportation–1966, Energy–1977, Education–1979, Veterans Affairs–1989.

Metacognitive Discussion

What information did you rely on to complete this activity? In what other circumstances does information like this help you?

Clue Card A

1. Our newest cabinet department was established in 1989.
2. Four cabinet posts were established in 1789. One was called the War Department, and another was called the Justice Department.
3. Henry Knox was the first secretary of the War Department. (The name "War Department" became defunct in 1949.)
4. There are 14 cabinet departments.
5. The Commerce Department and the Labor Departments were established exactly a decade apart early in the twentieth century.
6. All cabinet posts except one are held by an officer with the title of secretary.

Clue Card B

1. The Department of State is considered the oldest cabinet department.
2. Eight cabinet departments were established in the twentieth century.
3. The Commerce Department was the first cabinet department established in the twentieth century. It was established in 1903.
4. The Department of Energy was created before the Education Department and sometime after Housing in Urban Development (HUD).
5. Transportation was established 1 year after HUD and 17 years after the new Department of Defense.
6. Two departments were established in the nineteenth century; one of them was the Department of Agriculture.

Clue Card C

1. The Labor Department was established in 1913, and the Department of Health and Human Services was established 40 years later.
2. Exactly a decade after the thirteenth department was established, the fourteenth department was established.
3. The Treasury Department, Agriculture Department, and the Department of Veterans Affairs were established in different centers, 100 years apart from each other.
4. List the War Department and the Defense Department as one and the same.
5. The twelfth department was established two years before the next department (Education).

Clue Card D

1. The Department of the Interior was established exactly a century before the newly named Defense Department.
2. The department head usually is called the secretary of the department.
3. Because of the possibility of a terrorist act, the law requires that at least one cabinet member stay away from a gathering attended by the president.
4. The first three departments were established in 1789. The War Department was the second department established in that year.
5. Knox's department became the Defense Department in 1949.
6. Rank the cabinet departments according to the order in which they were established.
7. Alexander Hamilton, our first treasury secretary, influenced George Washington's fiscal policies.

SkyLight Training and Publishing Inc.

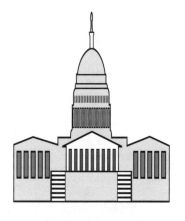

Apportionment

Activity 10

Since 1792, the House of Representatives has employed five methods to assign seats. Students should consult the handout "Congress's Methods of Apportionment, 1790 to 1990" (figure 2.2) and apply each method to complete a historical chart of membership numbers in the House of Representatives.

Background Information

Students need to understand the purpose of the census and the definition of an electoral vote.

The U.S. Constitution, Article I, Section 2, states: "The number of representatives shall not exceed one for every thirty thousand, but each state shall have at least one representative."

The Census Bureau conducts an official count of the American population every 10 years (decennial census) as specified by the constitution. The primary purpose the Founding Fathers attached to the census was to determine how to assign, or apportion, seats to the U.S. House of Representatives.

The apportionment or calculation of House of Representatives seats depends on three factors: first, the state's apportionment population; second, the number of representatives to be allocated; and third, the method used for the calculation.

The number of representatives a state has is based on that state's population. The total number of members of the House of Representatives has changed over the years. The House has used "Fixed Ratio" methods and "Predetermined Size" methods for determining the size of the House.

SkyLight Training and Publishing Inc.

The Reapportionment Act of 1929 fixed the permanent size of the House at 435 members.

The Constitution specifies that each state, regardless of the size of its population, is entitled to one seat. Fifty seats subtracted from 435 seats leaves a remainder of 385 seats; therefore, the current population of the United States is divided by the number 385. The result is the number of citizens who can be represented by one seat in the House of Representatives.

Each state is represented in the Electoral College. The number of a state's electoral votes is equal to its numbers of members of Congress. Each state has one electoral vote for each of its two U.S. senators and one for each member of the House of Representatives.

Objective

Students understand how the number of seats in the House of Representatives changed thoughout history as Congress used different apportionment methods.

Task

Students fill in the missing information in the table by using simple math to apply formulas in the handout "Congress's Methods of Apportionment, 1790 to 1990" (see figure 2.2).

Input

Refer to figure 2.1, Apportionment Through History, for information.

Metacognitive Discussion

When you change the way you do something, how do you evaluate the outcome?

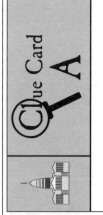

Clue Card A

1. The original method of determining apportionment began with the first census in 1790 and was used for 40 years.
2. There have been five methods used for determining the apportioning of seats in the House of Representatives.
3. In the Webster Method, if the remainder equaled one-half or more of the fixed-ratio number, the state would be granted an additional seat.
4. The Hill Method is also called the Equal Proportions Method.

Clue Card B

1. The Jefferson Method did not consider remainders, no matter how significant.
2. The Hamilton Method was also known as the Vinton Method.
3. The Webster Method was used for only two decades, as was the Major Fractions Method.
4. The Major Fractions Method was similar to the Webster Method, except fractional remainders were rounded using the arithmetic mean.

Clue Card C

1. The Hamilton Method was used for 50 years and preceded the Major Fractions Method.
2. The Webster Method replaced the Jefferson Method because it considered the fractional remainders.
3. With the Vinton Method, the House chose a predetermined number of representatives or seats and divided the population by that number to determine the value of one seat (e.g., House of Representatives = 220 seats).
4. If a seat = 30,000 people and the state's population is 105,000, a state would be granted four seats under the Webster Method but only three under the Jefferson Method.

Clue Card D

1. By the time of the 1990 census, the Hill Method of Apportionment had been used for 50 years.
2. The original method was called the Jefferson Method, and it used a fixed ratio of one seat for 30,000 people.
3. The Vinton Method came between the Webster Method and the Major Fractions Method.
4. The Webster Method used a fixed ratio similar to the Jefferson Method.

SkyLight Training and Publishing Inc.

Apportionment Through History
Student Worksheet

YEAR	Number of States	Number of Electoral Votes	Number of Representatives	METHOD OF APPORTIONMENT							
				Webster Method	Major Fractions Method	Hill Method	Vinton Method	Jefferson Method	Fixed Ratios	Remainders Considered	Fixed Seats Predetermined
1844	26	294									
1816	19	221									
1872	37	366									
1909	46	483									
1954	48	531									
1888	38	401									
1812	18	218									
1824	24	261									
1984	50	538									
1920	48	531									
1832	24	288									
1872	37	366									
1792	15	135									

SkyLight Training and Publishing Inc.

Congress's Methods of Apportionment, 1790 to 1990

1790 TO 1830
Jefferson Method
Fixed Ratio with rejected fractional remainders. A ratio of persons to representatives was selected (for example: 45,000 = 1 member of the House of Representatives). The population of each state was divided by this number. The whole number that resulted equaled the number of representatives a state had. Remainders were not considered, no matter how large they were.
Example: A state has a population of 300,000; at 45,000 per representative, the state will have six representatives at 270,000 and a remainder of 30,000. The 30,000 is not considered.

1830 TO 1840
Webster Method
Same as the Jefferson Method; however, the fractional remainders are considered. In the 300,000/45,000 example, the remainder of 30,000 is equal to a fraction of 2/3. In the Webster Method, anything over one-half would result in another seat being assigned. Thus the state would be assigned seven seats rather than six.

1850 TO 1900
Vinton or Hamilton Method
With this method, the House chose a predetermined number of representatives. For example, they could set the number of representatives at 180. The population then would be divided by this number to determine the value of an assigned seat. Any remaining seats then would be given to the states with the largest fractional remainders until all seats were distributed.

1910 TO 1930
Major Fractions Method
Similar to the Webster Method, fractional remainders were rounded using the arithmetic mean. The ratio determined would then be the predetermined size of the House.

1940 TO 1990
Equal Proportions or Hill Method
The Constitution specifies that each state receives one seat in the House of Representatives. The 50 states' seats are subtracted from the 435 total seats in the House, leaving 385 seats. The Equal Proportions Method uses a formula to establish a statistical ranking system to determine the order of allocation for the remaining 385 seats.

Figure 2.2

Apportionment Through History Answers

| | | | | METHOD OF APPORTIONMENT | | | | | | | |
YEAR	Number of States	Number of Electoral Votes	Number of Representatives	Webster Method	Major Fractions Method	Hill Method	Vinton Method	Jefferson Method	Fixed Ratios	Remainders Considered	Fixed Seats Predetermined
1844	26	294	242	✓					✓	✓	
1816	19	221	183					✓	✓		
1872	37	366	292				✓				✓
1909	46	483	391				✓				✓
1954	48	531	435			✓					✓
1888	38	401	325				✓			✓	✓
1812	18	218	182				✓		✓		
1824	24	261	213					✓	✓		
1984	50	538	435			✓			✓		
1920	48	531	435		✓		✓			✓	
1832	24	288	240		✓					✓	
1872	37	366	292	✓				✓	✓	✓	✓
1792	15	135	105								

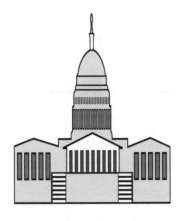

Apportionment: The Equal Proportions Method

Activity 11

Students calculate the values of House of Representatives seats and determine the order in which they will be assigned according to Congress's current method of apportionment, the Equal Proportions Method.

Background Information

This activity works best if students use a spreadsheet program; calculations by hand are possible, of course, but the process would be tedious and time-consuming. Students need to be familiar with using and entering formulas and equations in a spreadsheet program.

Objective

Students deduce the sequence of a spreadsheet formula, assign the correct number of seats in the House of Representatives to each state, and assign any remaining seats in the correct order.

Task

Students complete the House of Representatives Seat Numbers worksheet by using data on the "State Populations" handout and identifying, sequencing, and executing the steps in a spreadsheet formula for the Equal Proportions Method.

SkyLight Training and Publishing Inc.

Input

The seats to be assigned are as follows: 51–California, 52–Texas, 53–California, 54–New York, 55–Florida, 56–California, 57–Pennsylvania, 58–Illinois, 59–Ohio, 60–Texas, 61–New York, 62–California, 63–Michigan, 64–Florida, 65–California, 66–New Jersey, 67–Texas, 68–New York, 69–Georgia, 70–North Carolina.

The results of the spreadsheet formula or executions are shown in Figure 2.4.

Metacognitive Discussion

How long did it take you to write the formula? What helped you ensure the accuracy of your formula? What did you learn that will allow you to write formulas more accurately in the future?

Clue Card A

1. P = a state's population.
2. Indicate the number of the seats for each state that gained seats.
3. The current formula for apportionment calculation is the Equal Proportions Method (EPM).
4. There are currently 435 seats in the House of Representatives.
5. The Bureau of Census recommends multiplying up to the 60th seat to ensure all potential gains are covered.
6. In this particular problem, the spreadsheet formula for a square root equation can be written as follows: (1 / (N *(n-1))^.5).

Clue Card B

1. In this particular problem, the spreadsheet formula for a square root equation can be written as follows: (1 / sqrt (N *(n-1))).
2. The EPM was established to provide an equitable distribution of seats—based on population totals.
3. Create a spreadsheet program that shows the allocation of the remaining seats of the House of Representatives.
4. The Equal Proportion Method calls for the creation of a "multiplier" for each seat. The "multiplier" is created using the following formula: P * [1 divided by {the square root of N (N-1)}].

Clue Card C

1. Five formulas have been used by Congress for calculating apportionment at different times in the history of our country.
2. The Equal Proportion Method determines the order in which the states get seats 51 through 435.
3. Your program should include all 50 states and their populations (at least through 1996).
4. The fourth seat = 1/square root 4(4-1) = 0.28866751346.
5. Be certain to indicate which states have which number of seats (e.g., California has seats 51, 53, 56, and so on).

Clue Card D

1. All states get at least one seat in the House of Representatives.
2. The Equal Proportion Method creates a statistical ranking system to determine the allocation of the remaining 385 seats.
3. N = equals the number of the current seat in question. The second seat is N = 2; seat #3 is N = 3; seat # 14 is N = 14, and so on.
4. Spreadsheet Hint: Once you have a multiplier for one seat, copy and paste it to the next cell down (the next state), highlight the rest of the column for the other states, and "fill down."

SkyLight Training and Publishing Inc.

Equal Proportions Method/ Calculations

State	Population	Second Seat	Third Seat	Fourth Seat	Fifth Seat	Sixth Seat	Seventh Seat	Eighth Seat
California	31,878 ,234	22541315	13014234	9202210	7128189	5820142		
Texas	19,126,261	13524308	7808263.3	5521130	4276761	3491961		
New York	18,184,774	12858577	7423902.8	5249353	4066239	3320070		
Florida	14,399,985	10182327	5878769.2	4156807	3219934	2629065		
Pennsylvania	12,056,112	8524958.5	4921887.1	3480207	2695828	2201134		
Illinois	11,846,544	8376771.5	4836331.3	3419712	2648967	2162873		
Ohio	11,172,782	7900349.9	4561269.1	3225219	2498310	2039861		
Michigan	9,594,350	6784229.9	3916876.9	2769577	2145361	1751680		
New Jersey	7,987,933	5648321.5	3261059.9	2305856	1786156	1458390		
Georgia	7,353,225	5199515.2	3001941.5	2122637	1644231	1342509		
North Carolina	7,322,870	5178051.0	2989549.1	2113874	1637443	13369675		
Virginia	6,675,451	4720256.6	2725241.4	1926985	1492676	1218765		
Massachusetts	6,092,352	4307943.4	2487192.2	1758664	1362291	1112306		
Indiana	5,840,528	4129876.9	2384385.5	1685970	1305981	1066329		
Washington	5,532,939	3912378.6	2258812.8	1597179	1237202	1010171		
Missouri	5,358,692	3789167.4	2187676.8	1546880	1198239	978358.8		
Tennessee	5,319,654	3761563.4	2171739.6	1535611	1189510	971231.4		
Wisconsin	5,159,795	3648526.0	2106477.4	1489465	1153765	942045.3		
Maryland	5,071,604	3586165.5	2070473.6	1464007	1134045	925943.9		
Minnesota	4,657,758	3293532.2	1901521.7	1344543	1041506	850386.3		
Arizona	4,428,088	3131131.0	1807759.3	1278245	990150.5	808454.5		
Louisiana	4,350,579	3076323.9	1776116.4	1255870	972819.0	794303.4		
Alabama	4,273,084	3021526.6	1744479.2	1233500	955490.6	780154.8		
Kentucky	3,883,723	2746206.8	1585523.2	1121104	868426.8	709067.5		
Colorado	3,822,676	2703040.1	1560600.9	1103482	854776.3	697921.9		
South Carolina	3,698,746	2615408.3	1510006.7	1067707	827064.7	675295.5		
Oklahoma	3,300,902	2334090.1	1347587.5	952863.1	738104.1	602659.4		
Connecticut	3,274,238	2315235.8	1336702.0	945166.1	732141.8	597791.3		
Oregon	3,203,735	2265382.7	1307919.3	924814.2	716376.9	584919.3		
Iowa	2,851,792	2016521.4	1164239.2	823219.7	637680.0	520663.6		
Mississippi	2,716,115	1920583.3	1108849.3	784054.1	607341.7	495892.4		
Kansas	2,572,150	1818784.7	1050075.8	742496.1	575150.2	469608.1		
Arkansas	2,509,793	1774691.6	1024618.7	724495.7	561206.7	458223.4		
Utah	2,000,494	1414562.8	816698.25	577477.6	447324.0	365238.5		
West Virginia	1,825,754	1291003.0	745360.94	527035.8	408251.0	333335.5		
New Mexico	1,713,407	1211561.7	699495.47	494604.9	383129.4	312823.8		
Nebraska	1,652,093	1168206.1	674464.14	476905.5	369419.2	301629.5		
Nevada	1,603,163	1133607.4	654488.55	462781.0	358478.1	292696.1		
Maine	1,243,316	879157.17	507581.63	358904.9	278013.9	226997.4		
Idaho	1,189,251	840927.44	485509.68	343298.1	265924.6	217126.5		
Hawaii	1,183,723	837018.56	483252.89	341702.3	264688.5	216117.2		
New Hampshire	1,162,481	821998.19	474580.88	335570.4	259938.6	212239.0		
Rhode Island	990,225	700194.81	404257.66	285845.7	221421.0	180789.5		
Montana	879,372	621809.90	359002.11	253846.1	196633.5	160550.6		
South Dakota	732,405	517888.54	299003.08	211421.5	163770.7	133718.2		
Delaware	724,842	512540.69	295915.50	209238.3	162079.5	132337.4		
North Dakota	643,539	455050.79	262723.69	185768.8	143899.6	117493.6		
Alaska	607,007	429218.76	247809.57	175223.2	135730.8	110823.8		
Vermont	588,654	416241.23	240316.98	169925.2	131627.0	107473.0		
Dist. of Columbia	543,213	384109.59	221765.77	156807.9	121466.1	99176.67		
Wyoming	481,400	340401.20	196530.72	138964.5	107644.3	87891.21		

State Populations

STATE	POPULATION			STATE	POPULATION	
California	31,878,234			South Carolina	3,698,746	
Texas	19,126,261			Oklahoma	3,300,902	
New York	18,184,774			Connecticut	3,274,238	
Florida	14,399,985			Oregon	3,203,735	
Pennsylvania	12,056,112			Iowa	2,851,792	
Illinois	11,846,544			Mississippi	2,716,115	
Ohio	11,172,782			Kansas	2,572,150	
Michigan	9,594,350			Arkansas	2,509,793	
New Jersey	7,987,933			Utah	2,000,494	
Georgia	7,353,225			West Virginia	1,825,754	
North Carolina	7,322,870			New Mexico	1,713,407	
Virginia	6,675,451			Nebraska	1,652,093	
Massachusetts	6,092,352			Nevada	1,603,163	
Indiana	5,840,528			Maine	1,243,316	
Washington	5,532,939			Idaho	1,189,251	
Missouri	5,358,692			Hawaii	1,183,723	
Tennessee	5,319,654			New Hampshire	1,162,481	
Wisconsin	5,159,795			Rhode Island	990,225	
Maryland	5,071,604			Montana	879,372	
Minnesota	4,657,758			South Dakota	732,405	
Arizona	4,428,088			Delaware	724,842	
Louisiana	4,350,579			North Dakota	643,539	
Alabama	4,273,084			Alaska	607,007	
Kentucky	3,883,723			Vermont	588,654	
Colorado	3,822,676			Wyoming	481,400	

Figure 2.5

House of Representatives
Seat Numbers

Complete the chart by assigning the state to the corresponding seat number according to the priority set in the Equal Proportions Methods.

SEAT #51	SEAT #52	SEAT #53	SEAT #54	SEAT #55
SEAT #56	SEAT #57	SEAT #58	SEAT #59	SEAT #60
SEAT #61	SEAT #62	SEAT #63	SEAT #64	SEAT #65
SEAT #66	SEAT #67	SEAT #68	SEAT #69	SEAT #70
SEAT #71	SEAT #72	SEAT #73	SEAT #74	SEAT #75

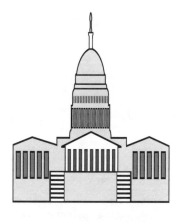

Gerrymandering a State

Activity 12

Students learn the concept of manipulating political district boundaries to ensure an election victory for a group. They create a visual representation of a fictional state and gerrymander its districts' borders to satisfy district population requirements. First they draw boundaries one way to empower one group; then they redraw them to favor the other!

Background Information

Gerrymandering is the practice of drawing political districts in such a way as to benefit or disenfranchise a particular political party, group, or candidate. Oddly shaped districts are usually the result of gerrymandering.

In gerrymandering, politicians use either of two techniques. With "packing," they draw district lines to include as many of a particular type of voter as possible to ensure that a certain party or candidate wins. Packing also effectively can limit a group or party to just one sure victory rather than two or more. Loading up just one district with a group prevents the group from being dispersed among—and winning elections in—two or more districts.

"Cracking" is the second technique. Politicians use cracking when they draw district lines to divide or dilute a group's power or voting strength. A group that could have won one seat if its members all could have voted in one unified district instead wins no seat at all.

SkyLight Training and Publishing Inc.

Gerrymandering has not been outlawed, but it happens with less frequency because of challenges in court. Redistricting, whether state or federal, comes under close scrutiny and occasionally results in a court invalidating a plan.

Objective

Students learn how gerrymandering affects citizens' representation in state government.

Task

Students draw and gerrymander a fictional state in several ways to satisfy district population requirements and to switch power from one group of voters to another.

Input

Among the possible options are four examples as shown in figure 2.7.

Metacognitive Discussion

What was hard about the assignment? How many techniques did you try? What helped you solve the problem? How can you use this experience to solve other problems like this in the future?

1. Your state is in the shape of a rectangle.
2. The population of your state is approximately 2,500,000.
3. Your state's population consists of two distinct groups.
4. The size of each of your political districts is 500,000 people.
5. Exercise 3: Draw the five political districts, as equally as possible, to ensure that there are at least three Lunarian winners and two Solarian winners.

1. Divide your state into 25 wards of equal size and population.
2. Identify each ward by using a symbol.
3. The Solarians are identified by the symbol S.
4. The Lunarians are identified by the symbol L.
5. Exercise 4: Draw the five political districts so that they might result in four Solarian winners and one Lunarian winner.

1. Each symbol represents about 100,000 people.
2. The group L controls 12 wards and the group S controls 13 wards.
3. Randomly distribute the two groups throughout your state. You may have one concentration area of a group, but place no more than 5 like symbols in that area.
4. The Solarians outnumber the Lunarians 1,300,000 to 1,200,000.
5. Exercise 1: Draw the five political districts to ensure that there is an equitable distribution of voters and that no group receives preferential treatment in as many districts as possible.

1. Solarians vote only for Solarian candidates and Lunarians vote only for Lunarian candidates.
2. Recreate the drawing of your state and its wards three more times.
3. Divide your state into five political districts of equal population (500,000 per district).
4. There is no guarantee that gerrymandered districts are of equal size (land area).
5. Exercise 2: Draw the five political districts, as equally as possible, to ensure that there are at least two Lunarian winners and three Solarian winners.

Gerrymandering a State
Worksheet

Exercise 1

S	S	S	L	L
S	S	L	L	S
S	L	L	L	S
L	L	S	L	S
L	L	S	S	S

Exercise 2

S	S	S	L	L
S	S	L	L	S
S	L	L	L	S
L	L	S	L	S
L	L	S	S	S

Exercise 3

S	S	S	L	L
S	S	L	L	S
S	L	L	L	S
L	L	S	L	S
L	L	S	S	S

Exercise 4

S	S	S	L	L
S	S	L	L	S
S	L	L	L	S
L	L	S	L	S
L	L	S	S	S

Gerrymandering a State
Answers

Exercise 1

Ⓐ S	S	Ⓑ S	L	Ⓒ L
S	S	L	L	S
S	Ⓓ L	Ⓔ L	L	S
L	L	S	L	S
L	L	S	S	S

Exercise 2

Ⓐ S	S	Ⓓ S	L	Ⓒ L
S	S	L	L	S
S	Ⓔ L	Ⓑ L	L	S
L	L	S	L	S
L	L	S	S	S

Exercise 3

Ⓐ S	S	S	Ⓒ L	Ⓑ L
S	S	L	L	S
Ⓑ S	L	Ⓓ L	L	S
L	L	S	L	S
L	L	S	S	S

Exercise 4

Ⓐ S	Ⓑ S	S	L	L
S	S	Ⓒ L	Ⓔ L	S
S	L	L	L	S
L	Ⓓ L	S	L	S
L	L	S	S	S

Figure 2.8

SkyLight Training and Publishing Inc.

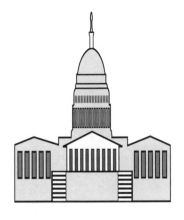

Gerrymandering a County

Activity 13

Students gerrymander a fictional county to change the power base of first one group of voters and then another.

Background Information

Refer to information on gerrymandering on pages 78–79.

Objective

Students learn how gerrymandering affects citizens' representation in local government.

Task

Students gerrymander a district to satisfy population requirements and switch power from one group to another.

Input

Following are possible solutions that will establish 5 districts with a population of 6,000 per district.

Plan A: Concede 2 districts to the town by putting 5,000 people in each district (using up the town's population), with 1,000 from the county going into each of these 2 districts—leaving 18,000 countians. who will form the remaining 3 districts.

Plan B: Concede 2 districts to the county by putting 6,000 people in each district (using up 12,000 of the county's population of 20,000, with 8,000 from the county being the remainder). Construct the remaining 3 districts by placing 3,333 town citizens in each of 2 districts and the remaining 3,334 in the third district.

Metacognitive Discussion

What are the advantages and disadvanages of gerrymandering?

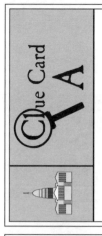

1. Those citizens living in the county number about 20,000 people.
2. All members of the Board of Supervisors run for election at the same time.
3. A precinct has at least 300 but not more than 350 people.
4. There are factions within the town that would like the town residents to control the decisions made by the Board of Supervisors.

1. Develop a plan (call it Plan B) whereby the town is able to control the majority of seats on the Board.
2. The county is divided into five political districts.
3. There are factions in the county that think the larger population of the county should mean that county residents have more control over the Board of Supervisors.
4. According to the "one person, one vote" principle, the five political districts should be equal in population.

1. One supervisor is elected from each political district.
2. Develop a plan (call it Plan A) whereby the county residents control the majority of seats on the Board of Supervisors.
3. The town usually is governed by a council.
4. Members of the Board of Supervisors are elected by popular vote.
5. The town encompasses 25 percent of the county's square mileage.

1. Identify the five political districts by the following names: Anderson, Blair, Cleaver, Dixon, and Emerson.
2. The town is divided into population zones called precincts.
3. The county's population also includes that of the town, which numbers about 10,000 citizens.
4. The Board of Supervisors controls the budget, decides on expenditures, and approves most major personnel decisions for the county.

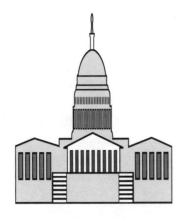

The Electoral College and the Election of 1824

Activity 14

Students count Electoral College votes in the one presidential election in U.S. history that was decided by the House of Representatives. Students who already know the outcome see the statistical story unfold before them. Have students who don't know the surprise ending research the winner of the 1824 presidential election. They will be especially intrigued as the teacher explains the Electoral College's role in the story.

Background Information

The students will need the following terms defined: electoral vote, popular vote, majority, and plurality.

The Founding Fathers thought it both impractical and undesirable to have the president elected by the total electorate. They created the Electoral College so that the people indirectly elect the president.

In the Electoral College system, the people actually vote for a candidate's slate of electors. These electors are pledged (but under no other legal obligation) to vote for the candidate under whose name they were listed. If the candidate/slate receives the most votes in the state's election, that candidate's/slate's electors cast their electoral votes in the state's capital on the second Wednesday in December.

The Electoral College never meets as a single body or organization; rather, it meets in 51 smaller bodies (the 50 states plus the District of Columbia). Unlike the voters in the popular election, Electoral College members vote separately for the president and for the vice president.

In six recent elections, at least one elector has cast his or her electoral vote for someone other than the person to whom he or she was pledged.

Four candidates ran in the 1824 presidential election. They were Andrew Jackson, senator from Tennessee; William H. Crawford, secretary of the treasury; Henry Clay, Speaker of the House; and John Quincy Adams, secretary of state. The election was a unique one in American politics and demonstrates a defect in the Electoral College. Jackson received the most popular and electoral votes, but not a majority, so the election was thrown into the House.

The result of the 1824 presidential race also shows the impact of having two or more strong candidates in an election when the Electoral College system is used.

Objective

Students learn how the Electoral College system worked in 1824.

Task

Students use deductive skills to fill in the Electoral College and the Election of 1824 chart to reveal the statistical story of the presidential election of 1824.

Input

Refer to figure 2.9.

Metacognitive Discussion

Were the Founding Fathers wise or unwise to mistrust a direct popular vote for the presidency? What are the responsibilities of those setting up a government for a new nation? How can this assignment help you to understand government decisions and their impact?

Clue Card A

1. A simple majority is defined as one more than half.
2. John Quincy Adams had 43 more electoral votes than did William Crawford.
3. The total number of House seats in 1824 was 213.
4. In the election of 1824, approximately 356,000 people cast their ballots.

Clue Card B

1. Jackson received about 43 percent of the popular vote.
2. Jackson received a plurality of the votes in both the popular election and the electoral election—as opposed to a majority of votes.
3. Adams received 32 percent of the electoral vote.
4. Citizens living in the District of Columbia were not included in presidential elections until ratification of the Twenty-third Amendment.

Clue Card C

1. Clay received 500 more popular votes than did Crawford.
2. Crawford was in third place in the electoral vote race but came in last as the people's choice.
3. In comparing Adams's acquisition of votes in the popular and electoral vote races, the difference was only 1 percent.
4. There were 24 states in the United States.
5. Jackson tallied 62 more electoral votes than did Henry Clay.

Clue Card D

1. Crawford's lead over Clay was two percentage points in the electoral race.
2. Crawford received 13 percent of the popular vote.
3. Only the top three candidates are considered by the House of Representatives.
4. Every state is guaranteed a minimum of three electoral votes. Each state has two U.S. senators and at least one representative.

Electoral College and the Election of 1824 Worksheet

Candidate	Number of Electoral Votes Needed to Win	Number of Electoral Votes Received	Percentage of Electoral Votes Received	Popular Votes Received	Percentage of Popular Votes Received
Andrew Jackson					
John Q. Adams					
William H. Crawford					
Henry Clay					

Figure 2.9

SkyLight Training and Publishing Inc.

Electoral College and the Election of 1824 Answers

Candidate	Number of Electoral Votes Needed to Win	Number of Electoral Votes Received	Percentage of Electoral Votes Received	Popular Votes Received	Percentage of Popular Votes Received
Andrew Jackson	131	99	38%	153,080	43%
John Q. Adams	131	84	32%	109,860	31%
William H. Crawford	131	41	16%	46,280	13%
Henry Clay	131	37	14%	46,780	13%

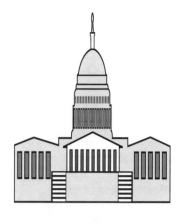

"Capitol" Murder: How to Kill a Bill

Activity 15

In a merry and fanciful way, this activity adopts a playful tone in detailing some of the ways a bill can die someplace on Capitol Hill and never become law. Students first meet one nonexistent character in the capitol and then eavesdrop on two others. Sam (the "Ax"), an investigator for Federal Bills Investigations, tells students that two operatives ("Mover" and "Shaker") are responsible for making much legislation vanish.

Younger students may need to be assured that no one is actually employed full-time in sabotaging American legislation.

Background Information

"The 'Hill' is a place where schemes and scams are the rule rather than the exception, and where promises are made and broken in almost the same instant.

"Some call me Sam, but I prefer my street name, 'Ax,' because I am known for bringing you down. I am an investigator on assignment for the FBI (Federal Bills Investigations).

"For years, most of the bills coming before the U.S. Congress have met with what I believe is foul play. I have been working for six months trying to uncover what is happening to most of the legislation arriving at our nation's capital. I believe that these bills met their untimely fate at the hands of two smooth operators, Mover and Shaker. The work of these two figures is responsible for thousands of deaths of bills each term of Congress.

"Take a look at the cases located in the Bureau of Missing Bills and see if you can match the Mover and Shaker with their

SkyLight Training and Publishing Inc.

individual techniques. I planted a listening device at Mover and Shaker's usual table in a Washington restaurant. Listen to what they're bragging about.

"I have theories on these and other cases. Read my Bureau of Missing Bills Status Report: Congressional Interviews Log Excerpts. After listening in on Mover and Shaker's conversation, come up with theories of your own about what they did to those bills. On each case, report to me the suspect and the weapon/tactic that person used."

Objective

Students understand ways that bills die in the congressional legislative process.

Task

Students draw up and complete a table of five fictional bills, the insider responsible for stalling or killing each, and the tactic used.

Input

The answers to this activity are provided in figure 2.13. Students will use the narratives found in figure 2.14 and match them with the information contained in the clue cards to unravel the mysteries on the "Hill."

Metacognitive Discussion

Which mystery was your team able to solve first? How did you/ they arrive at the solution? Did this lay the groundwork to solve the other mysteries or die each require a different process? Can this way of thinking be useful in other endeavors?

1. "My favorite method is to use the 'pigeonhole.' I just take the bill to committee and no one ever hears about it again."

2. "Shaker, I have a similar method. I just make certain that the bill is sent to a committee where it will not receive a favorable or welcome reception. If the chair doesn't like a particular bill, he or she will not bring it up."

3. "Yes, Shaker, 'by request' is a signal (from the sponsor/introducer) for everyone else to not bother with this bill . . . this signal makes my job very easy."

4. "I have taken a bill out right on the floor with a hundred people present simply by endless talking—I call it a filibuster, Shaker."

1. "Another place where I could strike is in the subcommittee or in the committee—by recording an unfavorable vote—which prevents the bill from moving on for future consideration—I have a lot of success with this method."

2. "Mover, tell me about the 'by request' technique that you use."

3. "Mover, I also get most of my targets in committee but occasionally some may make it out of committee. I'm sure you use the old technique of placing them somewhere on a calendar where they cannot even get on the floor for consideration."

4. "Shaker, you can send a bill onto the floor from a committee with an unfavorable or do not pass recommendation."

1. "A cute move to use after debate, but before a vote, is the 'recommit' trick. You should try it, Mover—send it back to a committee where you can start all over again!"

2. "Shaker, I know about a filibuster but I can't use it where I work—too many people present—almost 500 witnesses!"

3. "You can always get a bill by recording an unfavorable vote—especially if you use a roll call vote in which everyone has to state how they voted for the public record."

4. "You know, even if a bill makes it out of my house, it will be sent to your house! I know an expert like you will have all kinds of opportunities to get at it again."

1. "Mover, sometimes I can get the houses to disagree on the bill. Rather than work it out, they stay stubborn—and that's that!"

2. "Yes, I have even worked in 'command central'—I stop the bill by not signing it and daring anyone to do anything about it."

3. "Shaker, a subtle technique is to let them everyone in the houses go home and just keep the bill out of sight for 10 days—that's all it takes!"

4. "If all else fails, sometimes I connect with some lawyers and judges and get the bill declared unconstitutional. It can take years and years, but it's very effective."

Capitol Murder Table

Case	Suspect	Weapon/Tactic
1		
2		
3		
4		
5		

Figure 2.12

Capitol Murder Table Answers

Case	Suspect	Weapon/Tactic
1	Mover	Pigeonholing
2	Mover	Filibuster
3	Shaker	Recommit
4	Shaker	Veto
5	Mover	Do Not Pass

Figure 2.13

Bureau of Missing Bills Status Report: Congressional Interviews Log Excerpts

CASE 1

"My bill promoting a policy for free trade with China was sent to the House committee with old Chairman Russell presiding. The bill was introduced on the floor in May, and here it is November and I have heard nothing. I thought old Russell would be fair even though I knew the Korean War veteran was tough on communism."

CASE 2

"I hear two, possibly three, members of Congress are planning on holding up the vote on my bill by continuing debate indefinitely."

CASE 3

"My bill made it out of committee and onto the floor, but some consider it controversial because it includes language to ban the purchase of certain types of ammunition—most notably the cop-killing bullets. But now the bill has disappeared because of some fancy legislative maneuvering. I hear rumors that it's going back to committee for some revisions."

CASE 4

"All I know is that President Bentsen is adamantly opposed to my bill and will bully the members of his party if they oppose him."

CASE 5

"On its third time around, my bill made it out of committee, but people talked about its imminent doom. The only clue available was the initials D.N.P."

Figure 2.14

SkyLight Training and Publishing Inc.

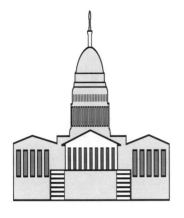

Coming to America

Activity 16

Students learn about the laws governing naturalization, the process of becoming a U.S. citizen after having been born in another country.

Background Information

Students need to understand the following terms: citizenship and alien.

Objective

Students learn how our naturalization laws apply.

Task

With reference to our naturalization laws, students rank fictional characters as to their citizenship or naturalization status and identify the requirements each character already has met or must meet in the future to be a U.S. citizen.

Input

1. Adelaide 2. Helen 3. Evan (Sammy's father) 4. Sammy
5. Isaac.

Eddie and Willie are already U.S. citizens.

Metacognitive Discussion

What are the benefits and disadvantages of naturalization requirements for a country? In general, do you think the United States' naturalization requirements are fair or unfair?

Clue Card A

1. Willie came to America at age 17 to play semi-professional baseball.
2. Article 1 Section 8 of the Constitution gives Congress the power to control naturalization.
3. The first federal naturalization law was passed in 1790 and allowed only free white persons who had been in the U.S. for two years to become citizens.
4. Naturalization laws require that an applicant be at least 18 years of age.
5. Helen arrived in the U.S. two years ago after marrying Eddie in London, England.

Clue Card B

1. Evan came to the United States to pursue an acting career three years ago.
2. Individuals over the age of 50 who have been permanent residents of the U.S. for 20 or more years are exempt from the requirement of demonstrating an understanding of the English language.
3. Today's naturalization laws are stricter than the laws in the 1800s.
4. Generally one is required to be a resident of the U.S. for a minimum of five years with at least half that time spent in actual residency in order to meet naturalization regulations.
5. Assume each of the characters speaks, writes, and reads English as is required by the laws of naturalization, with the exception of Adelaide who refuses to speak any language other that her native Gaelic.

Clue Card C

1. Adelaide, a fifty-five-year-old woman, immigrated to America at the age of 25. She lived in New York ever since.
2. The spouse of a U.S. citizen must be a resident of the U.S. for a minimum of three years before applying for citizenship.
3. A naturalized citizen has all the rights and responsibilities of any other citizen, except that he or she may not become President or vice-president of the United States.
4. All characters are of good moral character and are willing to take the Oath of Allegiance.
5. It wasn't until 1870 that a "person of African descent" could become a naturalized citizen.

Clue Card D

1. Isaac immigrated at age 18 but within two months the returned to Africa after his mother became ill.
2. He moved back to America last year at the age of 24.
3. Usually naturalization is done on an individual basis. However, in 1919 all residents of Puerto Rico were granted U.S. citizenship.
4. The Oath of Allegiance is administered to the applicant by a judge only after the applicant has proven to have met all naturalization requirements.
5. Willie turned pro this year after playing six years of semi-professional baseball in Florida. He has been signed by the Cleveland Indians.
6. After taking the Oath of Allegiance, an applicant and any of their minor children (under age 18) living in the U.S. become naturalized citizens.

SkyLight Training and Publishing Inc.

Economics

My Money, Our Money

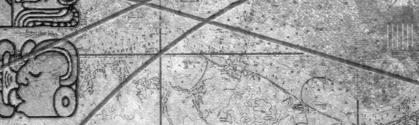

Economics:

My Money, Our Money

Teachers can use these activities in economics, business, math, marriage and family studies, civics, government, and American history courses.

Students participate in simulations of financial planning for corporations and young couples deciding to buy a home. Activities open up financial concerns of employers, employees nearing retirement, investors, taxpayers, home buyers, and home owners. There are no rose-colored glasses here!

Civics and government teachers will find the following real-world activities useful: "The IRS and the Single Taxpayer," "Social Security Retirement Benefits," "Watch Your Money Go!," and "Real and Personal Property Taxes."

Students write, enter, and run a spreadsheet formula for "Interest(ing) Times," "The Power of Diversification," "Social Security Retirement Benefits," and "Watch Your Money Go!"

In "Watch Your Money Grow," students learn about the world of finance and investment and advise fictional characters in investment decisions.

In "Family Matters," students are again placed in a simulation of being financial advisors. The students are asked to devise a financial plan to help the clients decide their course of action.

Teachers of tomorrow's home buyers can prepare them for financial planning and comparison shopping for mortgages with "Mortgage Smorgasbord," "To Buy or Not to Buy," and "Real and Personal Property Taxes."

Interest(ing) Times

Activity 17

Students learn the value of early investment and compounded interest.

Background Information

Students need to be able to write, enter, and run a spreadsheet formula.

Objective

Students learn the value of compounded interest and that well-timed (early) and consistent investing will net greater profits.

Task

Students write a spreadsheet formula and generate a spreadsheet to determine how much money two investors may expect to have earned from their investments by the age of their retirement.

Input

Paige invested a total of $18,000 and ended up with $579,468.02. Matthew invested a total of $70,000 and ended up with $470,249.45. (See Figure 3.1.)

Metacognitive Discussion

How did you arrive at your spreadsheet formula? What did you learn about sequencing the steps of a formula? What will you do differently the next time you write a formula? What did you learn about investing?

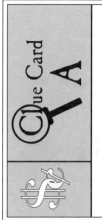

1. Wisely investing money will provide for future security.
2. Paige invested $2,000 a year for nine consecutive years.
3. Matthew began investing when he was 31 years old.
4. The Rule of 72 allows one to compute how long it will take to double your money at a given interest rate.

1. Matthew and Paige were born in the same year.
2. Paige began investing at age 22.
3. Once Matthew began investing, he faithfully contributed the same amount annually until he was 65.
4. The Rule of 72 tells you to divide the interest rate you are earning into 72 to determine how long it will take to double your investment.

1. To calculate the real rate of return of an investment, you must consider taxes and inflation.
2. Paige didn't contribute to her investment after she was 30.
3. Albert Einstein said, "The greatest force in the universe is the power of compound interest."

1. Paige invested her money at 9 percent interest annually.
2. Matthew invested $2,000 a year at 9 percent interest annually.
3. For the purposes of this activity, taxes and inflation will not be calculated.
4. Using a spreadsheet program and the clues provided, determine the total dollars invested by each investor and the total dollar amount available to each investor at age 65.

Interest(ing) Times

Paige

Age	Amount Invested	Savings Account	Interest	New Amount
22	$2000.00	$2000.00	$180.00	2180.00
23	$2000.00	$4180.00	$376.20	$4556.20
24	$2000.00	$6556.20	$590.06	$7146.26
25	$2000.00	$9146.26	$823.16	$9969.42
26	$2000.00	$11969.42	$1077.25	$13046.67
27	$2000.00	$15046.67	$1354.20	$16400.87
28	$2000.00	$18400.87	$1656.00	$20056.95
29	$2000.00	$22056.95	$1985.13	$24042.07
30	$2000.00	$26042.07	$2343.79	$28385.86
31		$28385.86	$2554.73	$30940.59
32		$30940.59	$2784.65	$33725.24
33		$33725.24	$3035.27	$36760.51
34		$36760.51	$3308.45	$40068.96
35		$40068.96	$3606.21	$43675.16
36		$43675.16	$3930.76	$47605.93
37		$47605.93	$4284.53	$51890.46
38		$51890.46	$4670.14	$56560.60
39		$56560.60	$5090.45	$61651.06
40		$61651.06	$5548.60	$67199.65
41		$67199.65	$6047.97	$73247.82
42		$73247.82	$6392.29	$79839.91
43		$79839.91	$7185.59	$87025.50
44		$87025.50	$7892.29	$94857.79
45		$94857.79	$8537.20	$103395.00
46		$103395.00	$9305.55	$112700.54
47		$112700.54	$10143.05	$122843.59
48		$122843.59	$11055.92	$133899.52
49		$133899.52	$12050.96	$145950.47
50		$145950.47	$13135.54	$159086.02
51		$159086.02	$14317.74	$173403.76
52		$173403.76	$15606.34	$189010.10
53		$189010.10	$17010.91	$206021.00
54		$206021.00	$18541.89	$224562.89
55		$224562.89	$20210.66	$244773.56
56		$244773.56	$22029.62	$266803.18
57		$266803.18	$24012.29	$290815.46
58		$290815.46	$26173.39	$316988.85
59		$316988.85	$28529.00	$345517.85
60		$345517.85	$31096.61	$376614.46
61		$376614.46	$33895.30	$410509.76
62		$410509.76	$36945.88	$447455.64
63		$447455.64	$40271.01	$487726.64
64		$487726.64	$43895.40	$531622.04
65		$531622.04	$47845.98	$579468.02

Matthew

Age	Amount Invested	Savings Account	Interest	New Amount
31	$2000.00	$2000.00	$180.00	$2180.00
32	$2000.00	$4180.00	$376.20	$4556.20
33	$2000.00	$6556.20	$590.06	$7146.26
34	$2000.00	$9146.26	$823.16	$9969.42
35	$2000.00	$11969.42	$1077.25	$13046.67
36	$2000.00	$15046.67	$1354.20	$16400.87
37	$2000.00	$18400.87	$1656.00	$20056.95
38	$2000.00	$22056.95	$1985.13	$24042.07
39	$2000.00	$26042.07	$2343.79	$28385.86
40	$2000.00	$30385.86	$2734.73	$33120.59
41	$2000.00	$35120.59	$3160.85	$38281.44
42	$2000.00	$40281.44	$3625.33	$43906.77
43	$2000.00	$45906.77	$4131.61	$50038.38
44	$2000.00	$52038.38	$4683.45	$56721.83
45	$2000.00	$58721.83	$5284.96	$64006.80
46	$2000.00	$66006.80	$5940.61	$71947.41
47	$2000.00	$73947.41	$6655.27	$80602.58
48	$2000.00	$82602.58	$7434.24	$90036.92
49	$2000.00	$92036.92	$8293.32	$100320.24
50	$2000.00	$102320.24	$9208.82	$111529.06
51	$2000.00	$113529.06	$10217.62	$123746.68
52	$2000.00	$125746.68	$11317.20	$137063.88
53	$2000.00	$139063.88	$12515.75	$151579.63
54	$2000.00	$153579.63	$13822.17	$167401.79
55	$2000.00	$169401.79	$15246.16	$184647.95
56	$2000.00	$186647.95	$16798.32	$203445.27
57	$2000.00	$205445.27	$18490.16	$223936.43
58	$2000.00	$225936.43	$20334.28	$246270.71
59	$2000.00	$248270.71	$22344.36	$270615.08
60	$2000.00	$272615.08	$24535.36	$297150.43
61	$2000.00	$299150.43	$26923.54	$326073.97
62	$2000.00	$328073.97	$29526.66	$357600.63
63	$2000.00	$359600.63	$32964.06	$391964.69
64	$2000.00	$393964.69	$35456.82	$429421.51
65	$2000.00	$431421.51	$38827.94	$470249.49

The IRS and the Single Taxpayer

Activity 18

Students learns about the progressive taxation system. The student are asked to find the tax rates from the information contained in the cards.

Background Information

The power to tax was the first power the U.S. Congress gave the government in 1789 when it ratified Article 1, section 8. Taxation is a way that a government can raise money for its use. Money brought in from an outside source is called revenue. Taxation also is a way a government can regulate economic activity and influence how individuals and businesses use resources.

The U.S. government gets most of its revenues by levying the personal income tax, which is a tax paid as a percentage of income. In the United States, it is a progressive tax, which means that as a person's income rises, his or her tax rate also can rise. This tax follows the ability-to-pay principle—those with higher incomes pay more in taxes than those with lower incomes. It does not matter whether or not the taxpayer uses the services offered by the government.

Objective

Students understand that U.S. citizens pay taxes on all money they accrue from any source.

Task

Students identify the three tax rates used by the IRS and the amount of the standard deduction for a single taxpayer.

Input

The tax rates are 15 percent, 28 percent, and 33 percent. The standard deduction for a single taxpayer is $4,150.

Metacognitive Discussion

How did you find the tax rates? Which facts helped you write the formula accurately? How can you spot similar facts in other problems?

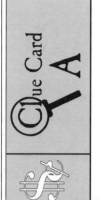

Clue Card A

1. All of the taxpayers in this activity are unmarried.
2. Taxpayer A earned $19,500 in 1992, and her income taxes came to $2,925.
3. In the year before his promotion, Taxpayer C paid $10,444 in income taxes because he earned $37,300.
4. Mary won a lotto prize worth $50,000, on which she paid $14,000 in taxes.
5. Larry won a lotto prize worth $1 million; after taxes the amount was $690,000.

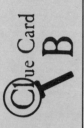

Clue Card B

1. The heavyweight champion's purse or winnings were estimated at $5 million. The IRS estimated that he would receive $3,450,000 after federal taxes were deducted.
2. The IRS uses three standard tax rates.
3. The highest tax rate also encompasses the largest window of income.
4. Student X worked various part-time jobs and earned a total of $21,642 last year. If she had earned just $192 less, her tax bill would have been $3,218; instead, her taxes for the year were $6,060.
5. The standard deduction is a flat dollar amount that is subtracted from the gross annual income of taxpayers who choose not to itemize their deductions.

Clue Card C

1. After using the standard deduction, Taxpayer A now owed $2,385 in taxes.
2. After using the standard deduction, Taxpayer C now owed $1,008 less for taxes.
3. Taxpayer L earned $51,900 and Taxpayer M earned $51,901—yet there was a difference of $1,557 in the taxes they paid. For taxes, Taxpayer L paid $14,532 and Taxpayer M paid $16,089.
4. The government agency that administers the charging and collecting of taxes is the Internal Revenue Service (IRS).
5. What is the amount of the standard deduction allowed for single taxpayers?

Clue Card D

1. After using the standard deduction, Taxpayer L owed $13,524 in taxes.
2. After using the standard deduction, Taxpayer M owed $13,524 in taxes.
3. Garry won a lotto game worth $5,000; after taxes, his prize was worth $4,250.
4. What are the three tax rates used by the IRS in assessing federal taxes on single people?
5. After six years with G Chip Electronics, Taxpayer C earned a promotion. On his new annual salary of $48,500, he paid taxes of $13,580.

SkyLight Training and Publishing Inc.

The Power of Diversification

Activity 19

Students learn the importance of spreading investments into different types of investment vehicles and different types of industry.

Background Information

Students need to be able to write, input, and run spreadsheet formulas.

Objective

Students understand the need to diversify investments.

Task

Students write, input, and run a spreadsheet formula to determine the end value of two investors' portfolios after 25 years.

Input

Michael earned $684,847.52. Ted earned $962,800.27. (See figure 3.2.)

Metacognitive Discussion

What kinds of products would you consider investing in? What are some other ways you are willing to spend your money? How much money should you allocate for your future . . . i.e. in savings, investments, etc.?

Clue Card A

1. Michael and Ted both have $100,000 to invest.
2. Ted decided to split his $100,000 into five separate $20,000 investments.
3. CD stands for certificate of deposit.
4. Financial advisors suggest that investors diversify their holdings by type of investment and type of industry.

Clue Card B

1. Ted bought $20,000 worth of stock in Technology Central Company, Inc.
2. Michael had a low tolerance for risk and needed an investment that would pay him a guaranteed return.
3. Ted bought a conservative bond issued by IBM that paid him 5 percent for 25 years.
4. Ted invested $20,000 in a local company, and over 25 years his investment never earned a dime. His principle never grew.

Clue Card C

1. Michael decided to invest $100,000 in a CD at a local bank for 25 years.
2. Ted invested $20,000 in a conservative domestic mutual fund that averaged an income of 10 percent a year.
3. Technology Central Company, Inc., went bankrupt and all its investors lost every cent of their investment.
4. Financial advisors suggest that when diversifying one's investment portfolio, one should consider diversifying by geographic locations as well as type of industry.

Clue Card D

1. Michael's certificate of deposit pays him 8 percent interest a year.
2. Every investment cited was for a 25-year period of time.
3. Ted bought $20,000 worth of an aggressive international stock mutual fund that had its ups and downs, but over the years averaged a return of 15 percent.
4. Determine the total amount of money available to each investor after the 25-year period.

SkyLight Training and Publishing Inc.

The Power of Diversification

Year	Michael's Investment #1 Savings* Interest	Savings + Interest
1	$8000.00	$108000.00
2	$8640.00	$116640.00
3	$9331.20	$125971.20
4	$10077.70	$136048.90
5	$10883.91	$146932.81
6	$11754.62	$158687.43
7	$12694.99	$171382.43
8	$13710.59	$185093.02
9	$14807.44	$199900.46
10	$15992.04	$215892.50
11	$17271.40	$233163.90
12	$18653.11	$251817.01
13	$20145.36	$271962.37
14	$21756.99	$293719.36
15	$23497.55	$317216.91
16	$25377.35	$342594.26
17	$27407.54	$370001.81
18	$29600.14	$399601.95
19	$31968.16	$431570.11
20	$34525.61	$466095.71
21	$37287.66	$503383.37
22	$40270.67	$543654.04
23	$43492.32	$587146.36
24	$46971.71	$634118.07
25	$50729.45	$684847.52

Year	Ted's Investment #1	Savings* Interest	Savings + Interest
1	$20000.00	$2000.00	$22000.00
2	$22000.00	$2200.00	$24200.00
3	24200.00	$2420.00	$26620.00
4	$26620.00	$2662.00	$29282.00
5	$29282.00	$2928.20	$32210.20
6	$32210.20	$3221.02	$35431.22
7	$35431.22	$3543.12	$38974.34
8	$38974.34	$3897.43	$42871.78
9	$42871.78	$4287.18	$47158.95
10	$47158.95	$4715.90	$51874.85
11	$51874.85	$5187.48	$57062.33
12	$57062.33	$5706.23	$62768.57
13	$62768.57	$6276.86	$69045.42
14	$69045.42	$6904.54	$75949.97
15	$75949.97	$7595.00	$83544.96
16	$83544.96	$8354.50	$91899.46
17	$91899.46	$9189.95	$101089.41
18	$101089.41	$10108.94	$111198.35
19	$111198.35	$11119.83	$122318.18
20	$122318.18	$12231.82	$134550.00
21	$134550.00	$13455.00	$148005.00
22	$148005.00	$14800.50	$162805.50
23	$162805.50	$16280.55	$179086.05
24	$179086.05	$17908.60	$196994.65
25	$196994.65	$19699.47	$216694.12

Year	Ted's Investment #2	Savings* Interest	Savings + Interest
1	$20000.00	$1000.00	$21000.00
2	$21000.00	$1050.00	$22050.00
3	$22050.00	$1102.50	$23152.50
4	$23152.50	$1157.62	$24310.12
5	$24310.12	$1215.51	$25525.63
6	$25525.63	$1276.28	$26801.91
7	$26801.91	$1340.10	$28142.01
8	$28142.01	$1407.10	$29549.11
9	$29549.11	$1477.46	$31026.56
10	$31026.56	$1551.33	$32577.89
11	$32577.89	$1628.89	$34206.79
12	$34206.79	$1710.34	$35917.13
13	$35917.13	$1795.86	$37712.98
14	$37712.98	$1885.65	$39598.63
15	$39598.63	$1979.93	$41578.56
16	$41578.56	$2078.93	$43657.49
17	$43657.49	$2182.87	$45840.37
18	$45840.37	$2292.02	$48132.38
19	$48132.38	$2406.62	$50539.00
20	$50539.00	$2526.95	$53065.95
21	$53065.95	$2653.30	$55719.25
22	$55719.25	$2785.96	$58505.21
23	$58505.21	$2925.26	$61430.48
24	$61430.48	$3071.52	$64502.00
25	$64502.00	$3225.10	$67727.10

Year	Ted's Investment #3	Savings* Interest	Savings + Interest
1	$20000.00	$3000.00	$23000.00
2	$23000.00	$3450.00	$26450.00
3	$26450.00	$3967.50	$30417.50
4	$30417.50	$4562.62	$34980.12
5	$34980.12	$5247.02	$40227.14
6	$40227.14	$6034.07	$46261.22
7	$46261.22	$6939.18	$53200.40
8	$53200.40	$7980.06	$61180.46
9	$61180.46	$9177.07	$70357.53
10	$70357.53	$10553.63	$80911.15
11	$80911.15	$12136.67	$93047.83
12	$93047.83	$13957.17	$107005.00
13	$107005.00	$16050.75	$123055.75
14	$123055.75	$18458.36	$141514.12
15	$141514.12	$21227.12	$162741.23
16	$162741.23	$24411.18	$187152.42
17	$187152.42	$28072.86	$215225.28
18	$215225.28	$32283.79	$247509.07
19	$247509.07	$37126.36	$284635.43
20	$284635.43	$42695.31	$327330.75
21	$327330.75	$49099.61	$376430.36
22	$376430.36	$56464.55	$432894.91
23	$432894.91	$64934.24	$497829.15
24	$497829.15	$74674.37	$572503.52
25	$572503.52	$85875.53	$658379.05

Family Matters

Activity 20

In the role of financial planners, students view a fictional family's financial situation and develop strategies for the family to adopt should they decide to make a career decision. They work with a handout, "Family Matters Financial Planner," client profile.

Background Information

Mr. and Mrs. Adams have two children, ages four and seven. Both parents are employed outside the home. Mr. Adams' employer is trying to persuade him to take a job in the company's Wisconsin office. His company promises to give him a $4,000 raise, buy their home in Florida, get the Adams started at the same point in a mortgage in a comparable new home, pay their moving costs, and help Mrs. Adams find a comparable job and salary.

The Adams are considering taking the offer, but they realize that maybe they have not managed their finances as well as they should have. Before making their choice, they decide to consult financial experts for a plan to follow if they elect to make the move.

Mr. and Mrs. Adams have heard of the snowy winters in Wisconsin and think they should buy a sport utility vehicle for Mr. Adams' business travels around the state. They own a ski boat and a motorcycle but no longer use them.

Objective

Students learn how a family with children, property, and debts considers a lifestyle decision that affects and is affected by its financial situation.

SkyLight Training and Publishing Inc.

Task

Students are financial advisors who examine and summarize a family's financial situation, recommend steps for the family to take if the couple should decide to move, and explain how their plan would accommodate the family financial condition (see figure 3.3).

Input

Students can be prompted to role-play, to act as financial advisors as a way to learn real-world skills for the workplace and adult life.

Metacognitive Discussion

How did the chart help you to organize the information? At what point did you realize you could offer a plan to the family?

SkyLight Training and Publishing Inc.

Clue Card A

1. Before taxes, Mr. Adams presently earns about $33,500 per year and Mrs. Adams earns about $27,500.
2. The Adams own a 1984 car. They owe five more monthly payments of $320 before they have completely paid for their 1993 car.
3. The personal property tax bill for both the motorcycle and ski boat is about $400 annually.
4. You are professional financial planners. Determine a financial plan for the Adams and list the steps you suggest they take if they should decide to take Mr. Adams' promotion, move to Wisconsin, and buy the sport utility vehicle.

Clue Card B

1. A new sport utility vehicle costs about $28,000. With no down payment, this vehicle financed at 60 months will cost about $590 per month; at 72 months the payments will run $540 per month.
2. The Adams family has a savings account with about $6,900 in it.
3. Insurance costs run about $650 per month, and their monthly grocery bill is around $400.
4. List the results for their family finances if the Adams follow your plan.
5. An asset is any item that a business or individual owns that has economic value.

Clue Card C

1. With all federal, state, and city income taxes assessed, the Adams are taxed at 28 percent.
2. The Adams spend about $75 per month on clothing and contribute $300 a month to their church.
3. Book value for the Adams' motorcycle is $4,600. The market value for the ski boat is $6,700.
4. Credit cards and revolving accounts run about $350 per month with a total balance of $4,800 to retire these debts.
5. The family sets aside $100 per month for savings and spends about $50 per month on family entertainment.

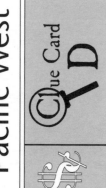

Pacific West

Clue Card D

1. Costs for all utilities, including fuel for the cars, total about $280 per month.
2. The mortgage payment for their Florida home is $650 per month with a balance of $34,900.
3. Personal property taxes are higher in Wisconsin than in Florida.
4. The Adams renovated their home and made some improvements about five years ago. They owe a second mortgage with a balance of $11,000 and a $475 monthly bill.
5. A liability is a debt of a business or individual.

Adams Family Finances

ASSETS

Motorcycle		$4,600
Ski Boat		$6,700
Savings Account		$6,900
Sport Utility Vehicle		$28,000
no down payment	5 years, 60 payments	$590
	6 years, 72 payments	$540

	Annual Income	Monthly Income
Mr. Adams	$33,500	$2,792
Mrs. Adams	$27,500	$2,291
Total		$5,083 before taxes
		$3,660 after taxes

LIABILITIES

	Monthly Payment	Balance Due
Utilities (water, power, heat, fuel)	$280	
Mortgage	$650	$34,900
Insurance (medical, property, life, car, boat)	$650	
Clothing	$75	
Groceries (food, lunches)	$400	
Credit Cards/Accounts	$350	$4,800
Loans	$475	$11,000
Car	$320	$1,600
Church	$300	
Personal Property Taxes	$400	
Total	$3,500	

OTHER EXPENSES

Saves	$100 per month
Family Entertainment	$50 per month

Family Matters Financial Planner, Client Profile

Account Executive _____   Date _____

City/State _____   Phone _____

FAMILY INFORMATION

Client/Spouse

Name (C) _____   (S) _____

Address _____   Home Phone _____

Employer/Occupation (C) _____   (S) _____

GOALS OR AREAS OF CONCERN

Increase cash flow now _____   Income at retirement _____

Educate children _____   Income tax reduction _____

Reduce debt _____   Sale of home/business _____

Sale of other major assets _____   Purchase _____

Other special considerations _____

INCOME

Taxable Earned Income (C) $ _____

Taxable Earned Income (S) $ _____

Non-taxable Income $ _____

Other Income $ _____

EXPENSES/LIABILITIES

Annual Federal Tax $ _____

Annual State Tax $ _____

Property Tax $ _____

Total Taxes $ _____

                                                              Balance

Mortgage $ _____ $ _____

Utilities $ _____

Car Payments $ _____ $ _____

Insurance $ _____

Food $ _____

Debts (Notes, Loans) $ _____

Debts (Credit Cards) $ _____

Debts (Accounts) $ _____

Miscellaneous Expenses $ _____

TOTAL EXPENSES $ _____

Figure 3.4

SkyLight Training and Publishing Inc.

Family Matters Financial Planner, Client Profile Flip Side

ASSETS

Savings /CDs	$ _____
Stocks	$ _____
Bonds	$ _____
Money Market Funds	$ _____
Life Insurance	$ _____
Personal Property	$ _____
Home Equity	$ _____
Money Market Funds	$ _____
IRAs	$ _____
Total Assets	$ _____

FINANCIAL DECISION

_____

_____

_____

_____

_____

_____

FINANCIAL DETAILS

	Amount	Reasoning
Transactions	$ _____	
	$ _____	
	$ _____	
	$ _____	
	$ _____	
	$ _____	
	$ _____	

Social Security Retirement Benefits

Activity 21

Students assume the role of a Social Security Administration employee who estimates retirement benefits for a person who has been employed steadily for 40 years.

Background Information

The students must have knowledge of how to input formulas and information into a spreadsheet program.

There are three major social insurance programs sponsored by our federal government. The government collects tremendous sums of money in taxes to fund Old-Age, Survivors, and Disability Insurance (OASDI); Medicare; and unemployment compensation. The IRS collects the revenues for these programs through individual workers' payroll taxes, called FICA taxes. Employers also make contributions to these social insurance programs by matching the amounts contributed by employees.

These three programs are referred to as "entitlements." Entitlements are benefits that must be paid to those who become eligible to receive them. Other entitlement programs include food stamps, veterans' pensions, Medicaid, and others.

OASDI is the oldest of the social insurance programs that were passed into law in 1935 in the midst of the Great Depression. This program is popularly referred to as Social Security. Social Security is not intended to completely finance one's retirement; rather, it is intended to provide some income for a person once he or she decides to work no longer.

The other features of OASDI are disability and survivors insurance coverage. The program provides disability income if one

116

becomes too disabled to work. If a spouse/parent dies and the survivors are eligible, a death benefit is paid to the family members until eligibility runs out. The formula given in this activity does not apply to disability or survivors insurance.

Objective

Students understand how the Social Security Administration calculates an individual's benefits.

Task

Students correctly sequence and follow the Social Security Administration's formula to calculate benefits and apply it to the wage history of a fictitious person.

Input

If Mr. Worker retires at age 62, he will receive $730.43 in monthly benefits. If he retires at age 65, he will receive $913.04 in monthly benefits (see Figure 3.6).

Metacognitive Discussion

How did you organize the steps to write the formula? What did you learn about sequencing the steps of a formula? What will you do better the next time you write a formula?

Clue Card A

1. To calculate benefits for retirement at age 62, multiply the amount calculated in step 6 by 80 percent. (This is the seventh and final step.)
2. Create and complete the rest of the data necessary for the table that shows the earnings of Joe Worker.
3. Joe Worker's request is submitted in February 1996. This estimate will be based on Joe's actual earnings through 1995.
4. Step 2: Fill in Column E by multiplying the amounts under Column B by the index factors in Column D.
5. The amount calculated in step 4 is called the average monthly index.

Clue Card B

1. Mr. Worker earned $3,000 in his first year of employment.
2. Mr. Worker's company gave him a salary increase of 6 percent for every year of employment after 1960.
3. Step 3: After adding the 35 years with the greatest amounts in Column D, complete step 4 by dividing this total by 420.
4. Any amount of the average monthly index above $2,741 is to be multiplied by 15 percent.
5. In 1960 Mr. Worker earned an income of $3,500.

Clue Card C

1. Use a spreadsheet program to complete Mr. Worker's profile.
2. The Social Security Administration's formula for calculating benefits for Mr Worker consists of seven steps.
3. If you work for wages, your employer reports the amount of earnings to Social Security after the end of each year.
4. For the first step, enter Joe Worker's yearly earnings in Column B.
5. You work for the Social Security Administration. Joe Worker (although not eligible) is curious about his potential retirement benefits at ages 62 and 65.

Clue Card D

1. Multiply the average monthly index between $456 and $2,741 by 32 percent.
2. Add the amounts calculated in the fifth step and round down to the nearest whole dollar to get the retirement benefits for Mr. Worker at age 65.
3. The earnings on the table should show the last full year worked.
4. The Social Security Administration bases benefits on earnings reported rather than actual taxes collected.
5. For the fifth step, multiply the first $455 of the average monthly index by 90 percent.

SkyLight Training and Publishing Inc.

Social Security Calculation Sheet

Year	Actual Earnings	Maximum Earnings	Index Factor	Indexed Earnings	Step 4 ($2028 – $455) $1573.56		
1957	$3000.00	$4200.00	6.78	$20340.00			
1958	$3000.00	$4200.00	6.72	$20160.00			
1959	$3500.00	$4800.00	6.41	$19230.00			
1960	$3500.00	$4800.00	6.17	$21595.00		$409.50	Step 5A
1961	$3710.00	$4800.00	6.05	$22445.50		$503.54	Step 5B
1962	$3932.60	$4800.00	5.76	$22651.78			
1963	$4168.56	$4800.00	5.62	$23427.28			
1964	$4418.67	$4800.00	5.4	$23860.81	Age 65	$913.04	Step 6
1965	$4683.79	$4800.00	5.3	$24824.08			
1966	$4964.82	$6600.00	5	$24824.08	Age 62	$730.43	Step 7
1967	$5262.71	$6600.00	4.74	$24945.23			
1968	$5578.47	$7800.00	4.43	$24712.61			
1969	$5913.18	$7800.00	4.19	$24776.21			
1970	$6267.97	$7800.00	3.99	$25009.19			
1971	$6644.04	$7800.00	3.8	$25247.37			
1972	$7042.69	$9000.00	3.46	$24367.70			
1973	$7465.25	$10800.00	3.26	$24336.71			
1974	$7913.16	$13200.00	3.08	$24372.54			
1975	$8387.95	$14100.00	2.86	$23989.55			
1976	$8891.23	$15300.00	2.68	$23828.50			
1977	$9424.70	$16500.00	2.53	$23844.50			
1978	$9990.19	$17700.00	2.34	$23377.04			
1979	$10589.60	$22900.00	2.15	$22767.64			
1980	$11224.97	$25900.00	1.97	$22113.20			
1981	$11898.47	$29700.00	1.79	$21298.27			
1982	$12612.38	$32400.00	1.7	$21441.05			
1983	$13369.12	$35700.00	1.62	$21657.98			
1984	$14171.27	$37800.00	1.53	$21682.05			
1985	$15021.55	$39600.00	1.47	$22081.67			
1986	$15922.84	$42000.00	1.43	$22769.66			
1987	$16878.21	$43800.00	1.34	$22616.80			
1988	$17890.90	$45000.00	1.28	$22900.36			
1989	$18964.36	$48000.00	1.23	$23326.16			
1990	$20102.22	$51300.00	1.17	$23519.60			
1991	$21308.35	$53400.00	1.13	$24078.44			
1992	$22586.85	$55500.00	1.08	$24393.80			
1993	$23942.06	$57600.00	1.07	$25618.01			
1994	$25378.59	$60600.00	1.04	$26393.73			
1995	$26901.30	$61200.00	1	$26901.30			
Indexed Earnings				$851995.41			
Average Monthly Indexed Earnings				$2028.56			

Watch Your Money Grow

Activity 22

Acting as investment advisors, students compare five fictional individuals' investments on the basis of a tax equivalent yield. Students learn how interest paid and taxes due on investments can affect the yield on an investment and how both state and federal investments are taxed.

Background Information

Students should understand the following terms: taxable equivalent yield, investment vehicle, tax investment vehicle, CDs, U.S. government bonds, municipal bonds, general obligation bonds, revenue bonds, and total taxable income. Review these terms after students finish the activity.

Students will use both the handout "State Income Taxes" and the clue cards, as well as information from the following scenario:

A wealthy couple who made their money in the retail business decided it was time to teach their grandchildren about the value of money. They gave each of their grandchildren $10,000 to invest for one year. Because this was their grandchildren's first "lesson" in investing, the couple limited their grandchildren's choices to three types of fixed-income investments: CDs, U.S. government bonds, or municipal bonds. The entire $10,000 had to be invested in only one investment vehicle. The grandparents planned to allocate their financial holdings to each grandchild based on the outcome of his or her investment strategies in this one year.

Certificates of Deposit (CDs) are issued by financial institutions, not government institutions, and all interest earned on such investments is subject to both state and federal taxes. The safest investment is a

SkyLight Training and Publishing Inc.

U.S. government bond because the government guarantees its bonds as opposed to merely insuring them. Municipal bonds are issued by state and local municipalities; they are also known as "muni's."

When comparing the interest rates on investments one must be sure to compare "apples to apples." A "before" tax rate is very different than an "after" tax rate.

Choose the best of the three investment choices for each of the grandchildren: Sean (single, age 26, living in Alaska with a taxable income of $55,000); Michael Patrick (single, age 25, living in Virginia with a taxable income of $32,000); Kelly (single, age 21, living in Vermont with a taxable income of $18,000); Mary Katherine (single, age 19, living in Arkansas with a taxable income of $20,000); and Danny (single, age 18, living in Florida with a taxable income of $18,000).

Objective

Students learn the yields and the tax consequences of investments.

Task

Students consult the handout "State Income Taxes" and the clue cards to decide on the best tax investment options for five unmarried people of different ages and incomes who live in different states.

Input

Refer to figures 3.7–3.9.

Metacognitive Discussion

Have you ever heard the saying "It's not how much you make but how much you keep?" What do you think about that? Do you know anyone who lives in an area that is either more expensive or less expensive than where you live? Why do such differences exist?

SkyLight Training and Publishing Inc.

Clue Card A

1. There are two types of municipal bonds—general obligation bonds (which are guaranteed by the government issuing the bond) and revenue bonds (which are not guaranteed).
2. Interest on municipal bonds (muni's) is considered an obligation of the state that issues the bond.
3. The primary benefit of owning muni's is their tax advantage.
4. The states of Virginia, Arkansas, and Vermont allow tax-exempt status for residents purchasing state bonds.

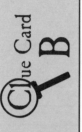

Clue Card B

1. In McCulloch v. Maryland, the Supreme Court ruled that the "power to tax is the power to destroy."
2. The states may not tax interest paid by the U.S. government on U.S. government investment offerings.
3. The U.S. government may not tax interest paid by the states on their municipal investment offerings.
4. Twenty-six of the 50 states give tax-exempt status to bonds purchased by residents of their state.

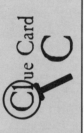

Clue Card C

1. In McCulloch v. Maryland, the Supreme Court ruled that the federal government may not tax state "obligations" and the states may not tax federal "obligations." (In the context of the case, "obligations" referred to the interest paid on investments.)
2. The IRS (Internal Revenue Service) uses three standard tax rates: 15 percent, 28 percent, and 31 percent.
3. When comparing interest rates on investments, always analyze the "taxable equivalent yield."
4. All of the grandchildren were able to find municipal bonds in their respective states paying 7 percent interest annually.

Clue Card D

1. If your total taxable income is at or below $21,450, your tax rate is 15 percent.
2. If your total taxable income is between $21,451 and $51,900, your tax rate is 28 percent. If your taxable income is over $51,900, your tax rate is 31 percent.
3. To calculate the "taxable equivalent yield," use the following formula: Divide the interest rate that your bond is paying by 100 minus your tax rate.
4. The interest rate paid on U.S. government bonds currently is 9 percent annually.
5. The best rate that any of the grandchildren were able to obtain on a 12-month CD was 9.5 percent.

SkyLight Training and Publishing Inc.

Watch Your Money Grow

Grandchildren	CD*	U.S. Government Bond	Municipal Bond
Michael Patrick			
Sean			
Kelly			
Mary Katherine			
Danny			

*CD = certificate of deposit

Figure 3.7

Watch Your Money Grow Answers

Grandchildren	CD	U.S. Government Bond	Municipal Bond
Michael Patrick	9.5	9	10.1*
Sean	9.5	9.89	11.3*
Kelly	9.5	9.67*	9
Mary Katherine	9.5	9.49	10.5*
Danny	9.5*	9	8.2

Figure 3.8

State Income Taxes

STATE	RATE	STATE	RATE	STATE	RATE
Alabama	5.0%	Louisiana	6.0%	Ohio	7.5%
Alaska	None	Maine	8.5%	Oklahoma	7.0%
Arizona	7.0%	Maryland	8.0%	Oregon	9.0%
Arkansas	7.0%	Massachusetts	5.95%	Pennsylvania	2.8%
California	11.0%	Michigan	4.4%	Rhode Island	11.0%
Colorado	5.0%	Minnesota	8.5%	South Carolina	7.0%
Connecticut	4.5%	Mississippi	5.0%	South Dakota	None
Deleware	7.7%	Missouri	6.0%	Tennessee	6.0%
Florida	None	Montana	11.0%	Texas	None
Georgia	6.0%	Nebraska	6.99%	Utah	7.2%
Hawaii	10.0%	Nevada	None	Vermont	9.0%
Idaho	8.2%	New Hampshire	5.0%	Virginia	5.75%
Illinois	3.0%	New Jersey	6.65%	Washington	None
Indiana	3.4%	New Mexico	8.5%	Washington, D.C.	9.5%
Iowa	9.98%	New York	7.5%	West Virginia	6.5%
Kansas	6.0%	North Carolina	7.75%	Wisconsin	6.93%
Kentucky	6.0%	North Dakota	12.0%	Wyoming	None

Figure 3.9

Watch Your Money Go!

Activity 23

Note: Computers/a spreadsheet program are needed for this activity.

Students deduce and assemble tax tables similar to those of the IRS and comprehend the workings of its progressive taxation system.

Background Information

Students need to be able to write, input, and run a spreadsheet program.

Objective

Students understand how a progressive taxation system works.

Task

The students deduce the content and sequencing of a spreadsheet formula to create tax tables similar to those found in IRS 1040 publications.

Input

Refer to figure 3.10.

Metacognitive Discussion

How did you arrive at your spreadsheet formula? What did you learn about sequencing the steps of a formula? What will you do better the next time you write a formula?

1. Write a spreadsheet program to create a tax table.
2. The tax table begins at $0.00 income.
3. The final bracket begins at $49,000.
4. Inside the third bracket, any amount of income earned over $49,000 is taxed at the third bracket rate and added to the initial tax imposed.

1. The table will reflect three brackets.
2. Show income in $500 increments or levels.
3. The table will reflect three tax rates.
4. In the third income bracket, an initial tax of $13,162 is imposed.
5. Inside the first bracket, each level is taxed at the first percentage rate.

1. After $24,000, the tax rate jumps 13 percentage points to 28 percent.
2. The ceiling on the income represented in this table is $80,000.
3. The tax rates are of unequal percentage jumps.
4. A new level begins at $1 above the maximum value of the previous level.
5. Calculate values for the tax tables by using a spreadsheet.

1. The final tax rate is 18 points higher than the initial rate.
2. Inside the second income bracket, an initial tax of $3,600 is imposed.
3. Tax at the value that reflects the midway point of a level (e.g., if a level is 0–10, the midway point is 5).
4. Inside the second bracket, any amount of income earned over $24,000 is taxed at the second bracket rate and added to the initial tax imposed.

Watch Your Money Go! Tax Table

Step 1   You will probably need a minimum of 15 columns and 51 rows. The column headings will be: Column #A) "Your income is at least"; Column #B) "But not more than"; Column #C) "Your tax is"; Column #D) a blank column used to separate brackets (no entries and no headings!). One could copy and paste this sequence across the first row (Row 1) of cells in the program until all 15 columns now have these headings. (Columns E, F, G; I, J, K; and M, N, O should have these same headings.)

Step 2   In the second cell (Row 2) under Column A, enter the dollar amount "$0.00"
In the second cell (Row 2) under Column B, enter the dollar amount "$500.00"
In the second cell (Row 2) under Column C, enter the following formula "=B2*.15"

Step 3   In the third cell (Row 3) under Column A, enter the formula "=A2 + 501"
In the third cell (Row 3) under Column B, enter the formula "=B2 + 500"
In the third cell (Row 3) under Column C, enter the following formula "=(B3 + 250)*.15"

Step 4   In the fourth cell (Row 4) under Column A, enter the formula "=A2 + 500"
In the fourth cell (Row 4) under Column B, enter the formula "=B3 + 500"
In the fourth cell (Row 4) under Column C, enter the following formula "C2[=(B4 + 250)*.15" and paste.

Step 5   For the fifth cell down (Row 5), Column A, highlight A4 and copy; highlight A4 again and the rest of the column down to A51; and execute a "fill down" manuever.
For the fifth cell down (Row %), Column B, highlight B4 and copy; highlight the column down to B51; and execute a fill down.
For the fifth cell down (Row 5), Column C, highlight C4 and copy; highlight the column down to C51; and execute a fill down.

Step 6   For Columns E, F, G
In cell E2, enter the amount $24,501. In cell F2, enter the amount $25,000.
In cell G2, enter the following formula =((E2 + 250 - 24000) * .28) + 3600. Highlight G2 and copy; highlight G2 again and the rest of the column down to G51; and execute a fill down. In cell E3, enter the formula = E2 + 500, execute a copy and a fill down.
In cell F3, enter the formula = E2 + 500, execute a copy and a fill down.

Step 7   For Columns I, J, K
In cell I2, enter the amount $49,001. In cell J2, enter the amount $49,500.
In cell K2, enter the following formula =((I2 + 250 - 49000) * .33) + 13160. Highlight K2 and copy; highlight K2 again and the rest of the column down to K51; and execute a fill down. In cell I3, enter the formula = I2 + 500, execute a copy and a fill down.
In cell J3, enter the formula = J2 + 500, execute a copy and a fill down.

Step 8   For Columns M, N, O
In cell M2, enter the amount $73,500. In cell N2, enter the amount $74,000.
In cell O2, enter the following formula =((M2 + 250 - 73500) * .33) + 13160. Highlight O2 and copy; highlight O2 again and the rest of the column down to O14($80,000); and execute a fill down.
In cell M3, enter the formula = M2 + 500, execute a copy and a fill down.
In cell N3, enter the formula = N2 + 500, execute a copy and a fill down.

Figure 3.10

Mortgage Smorgasbord

Activity 24

Students learn about several types of mortgages and the long-term obligations they impose.

Background Information

Students should understand such terms as mortgage, interest, fixed rate, cap, interest-rate index, T-bill, and equity before doing this activity.

Objective

Through a simulation of the home-buying process, students comprehend ramifications of a long-term financial obligation they may assume in adult life, and explore options before making an either-or choice in a high-cost arena.

Task

Students project long-term financial obligations of a fictional couple's limited options and explain their recommendations for a mortgage best suited for the couple.

Input

Students again can be prompted to role-play as real-world financial advisors and consumers.

Metacognitive Discussion

As you were working, were you aware of any new knowledge you were acquiring? Did any new information cause you to form a new position on a brand-new subject in your life? Did any new information cause you to rethink a former position?

SkyLight Training and Publishing Inc.

Clue Card A

1. Adjustable rate mortgages (ARMs) have flexible interest rates that vary according to time and a selected interest-rate index (usually a T-bill index). The interest rate on an ARM loan may go up or down every time it adjusts.
2. A graduated payment mortgage (GPM) is a fixed-rate mortgage, although the monthly payment amount is not fixed. The monthly payment varies over time, generally with lower payments at the beginning of the loan and higher payments as the loan matures. This type of loan allows buyers to qualify more easily for a mortgage loan.
3. Michael and Megan found a GPM with an interest rate of 8.5 percent for 30 years. Monthly payments start $100 less than those of a conventional loan of 7 percent for 30 years.
4. Michael and Megan want a mortgage with the lowest monthly payment with the least amount of risk.

Clue Card B

1. Michael and Megan have found a fixed-rate 30-year mortgage at 8 percent.
2. They have also found a 15-year fixed-rate mortgage at 7.5 percent.
3. Fixed-rate mortgages have an interest rate that remains constant throughout the term of the loan.
4. A "wrap-around mortgage" allows a buyer to assume the seller's mortgage and add in a new loan to total the money needed to complete the sale.
5. When considering an ARM, be sure to check how much the interest rate can change each time the loan "adjusts." Also, check whether there is a cap on the amount that the interest rate can change over the life of the loan.

Clue Card C

1. Assume an existing loan greatly reduces the "up front" costs of buying a home.
2. Michael and Megan found a 1-year ARM with an interest rate of 5.75 percent. This loan has a 2 percent annual cap and a lifetime cap of 6 percent. This means their loan is evaluated every year and their interest rate may change as much as 2 percent. The interest rate on this loan can change as much as 6 percent over the life of the loan but no more. In other words, their interest rate could increase up to a maximum of 11.75 percent within 3 years.
3. Michael anticipates getting a promotion and working at his company's home office within the next four years. It would mean that he and Megan would move from their present location of Canton, Ohio, to Dallas, Texas.
4. Mortgage loans are not always assumable.

Clue Card D

1. Assumable loans are attractive only when the interest rate of the old loan is below the current market rates.
2. Michael and Megan found a two-step loan at the rate of 7 percent for the first seven years and the rate of $8^1/4$ percent for the remaining 23 years of the loan.
3. The house Michael and Megan are most interested in does not have an assumable mortgage.
4. A "two-step" loan, sometimes is known as a 7/23, is a fixed-rate loan. For the first seven years of the loan, the interest is fixed at a rate that generally is below the market rate. For the next 23 years, the interest rate is fixed at a higher-than-market rate.
5. A one-year ARM is a loan that adjusts every year. This adjustment can raise or lower the monthly payments depending on whether the interest rate is adjusted up or down. A three-year ARM can only adjust or change every three years.

SkyLight Training and Publishing Inc.

To Buy or Not to Buy

Activity 25

Students learn the terms under which potential borrowers qualify for a mortgage, establish whether a fictional couple can afford one, and figure out the costs of points and closing costs.

Background Information

Terms such as points, equity, lender, collateral, qualifying ratios, and appreciation should be covered before assigning this activity.

Objective

In a simulation of the home-buying process, students learn the importance of good personal financial and employment practices. They project costs of long-term loans repaid with interest and of various monthly payments budgeted from annual salaries. They experience deciding whether a long-term obligation should be assumed, and learn of home-buying costs they may not have anticipated.

Task

Students assess a fictional couple's credit, earnings, savings, and work history to determine whether the couple will qualify for a loan. They also decide whether the couple can afford the monthly payments of either of two available mortgages. Students select the mortgage in the couple's best interest and derive the points and closing costs of the loan.

Metacognitive Discussion

How did you organize the information? When did you realize you could recommend a specific mortgage to the couple?

SkyLight Training and Publishing Inc.

Clue Card A

1. The house Michael and Megan want to buy is priced at $100,000. Their realtor has indicated the true value of the home is somewhere around $110,000, but the sellers are anxious to sell.

2. Generally, a person must be employed in the same line of work for a minimum of six months in order to qualify for a mortgage loan.

3. Mortgage loans are loans that finance real estate. The real estate is used as collateral for the loan.

4. A point is 1% of the loan amount. Lenders usually charge 1 "discount point" and 1 "point" to cover what is termed the loan origination fee or up-front costs of processing the loan. This commonly practiced formula is known as 1+1.

5. Lending institutions offer conventional loans for various lengths of time. The most common mortgage terms are for 15 or 30 years.

Clue Card B

1. Michael and Megan have saved $12,000 to cover the down payment and closing costs on their house.

2. Closing costs usually run about 5% of the sales price of the home. They include appraisal cost, attorney fees, inspections, and recording fees.

3. It is possible to obtain mortgage financing without paying any points, but the interest rate will be higher. For example, the interest rate on a 30-year mortgage might be half of one percentage point higher on a 0+0 loan than on a 1+1 loan.

4. The monthly cost of PMI on a $95,000 loan is $48.

5. Defaulting on a loan means not making payments on schedule as agreed.

6. Michael earns $35,000 a year. Megan works part-time and earns $15,000 a year.

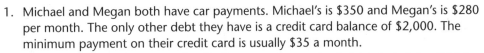

Clue Card C

1. Michael and Megan both have car payments. Michael's is $350 and Megan's is $280 per month. The only other debt they have is a credit card balance of $2,000. The minimum payment on their credit card is usually $35 a month.

2. When a mortgage loan is made, the borrower signs a deed of trust pledging that the property will revert back to the lending institution in case the borrower defaults.

3. Lenders use qualifying ratios to determine whether a loan should be made or not. The qualifying ratios for a conventional loan are 28 and 36. This means a person's house payment may not exceed 28% of his or her gross monthly earnings, and a person's total debt (mortgage payment, car payments, credit cards payments, etc.) may not exceed 36% of his or her gross monthly earnings.

4. Generally, it takes 30 to 45 days to complete a sale of a home from the time of making a written offer to buy to the closing (signing and recording of all documents).

Clue Card D

1. Michael and Megan's credit report shows an excellent credit rating.

2. The monthly payment on a loan of $95,000 for 30 years at 8% is $697.08 excluding PMI.

3. The monthly payment on a loan of 95,000 for 15 years at 7.5% is $880.66 excluding PMI.

4. Both Michael and Megan have been at their present jobs for over two years.

5. If your equity (down payment and/or appreciation) in the property is less than 20 percent, the lending institution will require you to purchase mortgage insurance.

6. Private mortgage insurance (PMI) costs are added to your monthly payment amount and are included in calculating qualifying ratios.

Real and Personal Property Taxes

Activity 26

Students learns about local taxes on homes, vehicles, trailers, and boats.

Objective

Students learn about how a local property tax system works.

Task

Students compute three fictional couples' real and personal property taxes for inclusion on a chart.

Input

Refer to figures 3.11 and 3.12.

Metacognitive Discussion

How did you organize the information? At what point did you realize you were going to solve the problem?

SkyLight Training and Publishing Inc.

1. The Relifords' personal property tax assessment was based on a 1994 automobile valued at $25,000 and a 1996 sport utility vehicle valued at $28,000.
2. Tangible personal property can be seen, is movable, and can be easily assessed. Examples are cars, mobile trailers, and boats.
3. Homes are considered real property.
4. Assessment is the process of determining the value of the property to be taxed.

1. The O'Donnells owned a boat and a Jeep collectively valued at $37,000. Their personal property tax bill was $735.
2. The Laws owned just one vehicle, and they had to pay a personal property tax bill of $312.
3. Fill in the missing values on the chart.

1. The Relifords' personal property tax bill was $60 more than the O'Donnells' personal property tax bill.
2. Intangible personal property such as stocks, bonds, and bank accounts can be more easily hidden, so many states do not bother to tax them.
3. The real property tax rate is exactly one-half the personal property tax rate anywhere in the United States.

1. A property tax bill can rise for several reasons: (1) the value of a property rises; (2) a locality increases the tax rate; and/or (3) a periodic planned reassessment occurs.
2. The O'Donnells paid a total of $1,972.50 in taxes on their real property and personal property.
3. The Laws' real property tax bill was $937.50.
4. The tax assessor taxes at 100 percent the appraised value of the property.

Property Tax Problem-Solving Activity

	Families	Vehicle #1	Vehicle #2	Personal Property Tax Bill	Personal Property Tax Rate per $100	Real Value of Real Estate	Real Property Tax Bill	Property Tax Rate/$100	Total Tax Bill

Figure 3.11

SkyLight Training and Publishing Inc.

Property Tax Problem-Solving Activity

Families	Vehicle #1	Vehicle #2	Personal Property Tax Bill	Personal Property Tax Rate per $100	Real Value of Real Estate	Real Property Tax Bill	Property Tax Rate/$100	Total Tax Bill
O'Donnells	$37,000.00	$12,000.00	$735.00	$1.50	$165,000.00	$1,237.50	$0.75	$1,972.50
Relifords	$28,000.00	$25,000.00	$795.00	$1.50	$227,200.00	$1,704.00	$0.75	$2,499.00
Laws	$20,800.00	—	$312.00	$1.50	$125,000.00	$ 937.50	$0.75	$1,249.50

Figure 3.12

SkyLight Training and Publishing Inc.

PART IV

Cultures

Mystery from History

Cultures:

Mystery from History

History, government, literature, marriage and family, math, computer, and geography teachers can use Part IV activities to supplement coursework.

For the two "Succession to the British Throne" and the two "Royal Surfing" activities, teachers assign research and assembly of genealogical charts and introduce students to the differing rules of succession in three Western monarchies.

Although the late-eighteenth century family used in "Succession to the British Throne" is fictional, the rules of succession are sound. Literature teachers will find these activities helpful in introducing Shakespeare and explaining character motive. Teachers of British and European history and government can use both to explain royal succession in this once-powerful empire. Marriage and family teachers can use them to introduce genealogical charting and demonstrate inheritance patterns.

The European dynasties that are the topics of the two "Royal Surfing" activities are real. Both activities require that students surf the Net and can use Internet search engines. Computer skills teachers can assign these Internet research activities for practice. History teachers focusing on twentieth-century Belgium and Norway can assign Parts 1 and 2, respectively. Government and geography teachers can use these activities to supplement European studies, and marriage and family teachers can use them to introduce genealogical charting and demonstrate inheritance patterns.

Math teachers can use "Roman Numerals" to introduce or reinforce a working knowledge of that counting system. Teachers in general can use the "Roman Numerals" activity as a bridge to the two "Mayan Math" activities, which introduce students to the Mayan counting system, which uses vertical stacking, three symbols, a base of 20, and zero. Explain to students that the Mayan counting system is not commonly used today. Intrigue them by telling them that the Maya of the Classic Era inexplicably vanished over a thousand years ago, although their descendents still live in Mexico and Central America today. Math teachers can skip Parts 1 and 2 of "Search for the Zytar" and assign Part 3, in which students crack the code to translate a fictional message on a Mayan temple wall.

Geography, government, and history teachers can assign Parts 1 and 2 of the "Search for the Zytar" activities. Although the story line about the Zytar is fictional, the information about the Incan, Aztecan, and Mayan civilizations is true. Geography teachers can assign these activities to supplement Central American studies, government teachers can use them as examples of empires and city-states, and history teachers can use them as an overview of Central America from the third to the sixteenth centuries. It is not necessary to complete the trilogy; however, if geography, government, and history teachers wish to assign Part 3, they need to ensure that students first successfully complete both "Mayan Math" activities.

SkyLight Training and Publishing Inc.

Activity 27

Succession to the British Throne (Part 1)

Students learn to construct a genealogical chart and order the line of succession for members of a fictional eighteenth-century British monarchy.

Background Information

Students need to be shown a genealogical chart and understand that it delineates a family's biological relationships through generations. Such a chart is a chronological listing, by name, of each person born to a family member, and includes dates of all known births, deaths, and marriages.

Genealogical charts are useful not only for personal interest but also for determining inheritance (whether of property, status, or genetics). A chart tracing several generations through either the mother or the father is more easily understood than one that tries to trace through both simultaneously. A chart traced through either mother or father is true to genealogy.

The following information is useful for completing Parts 1 and 2 of "Succession to the British Throne."

In Great Britain's hereditary monarchy, only a person born into the royal family can become the country's monarch (a king or a queen regnant). A monarch remains the monarch until his or her death or abdication. A woman who is titled a queen is either a queen regnant or a queen consort. A queen regnant is a reigning monarch because she is a direct descendent of a monarch and has all the duties and rights of one. It does not matter whether a queen regnant is married or not. A queen consort is queen only as long as she is married to a king.

In this hereditary monarchy, succession historically is determined with bias by both gender (males precede females) and order of birth (the elder precedes the younger). In every instance described below, sons rank higher in the line than daughters, elder sons rank higher than younger sons, and elder daughters rank higher than younger daughters.

In the line of royal succession, a person's position moves backward with the birth of anyone closer to the throne and forward with the death of such an individual.

Succession when the British monarch has children: All the children are in direct line for the throne according to gender and birth-order bias. If the monarch has three daughters A, B, and C, born before three sons D, E, and F, the order of succession (before any of them have children of their own) is D-E-F-A-B-C.

Succession when the British monarch has grandchildren: Each grandchild ranks immediately behind his or her parent according to the prevailing gender and birth-order bias. For the D-E-F-A-B-C example, all of D's children rank higher in the line of succession than their uncles E and F and their aunts A, B, and C. All of E's children rank higher than their uncle F and their aunts A, B, and C, and so on.

Succession when the British monarch has no children: The monarch's brothers are in line for the throne according to their order of birth, followed by the monarch's sisters according to their order of birth. Each of the monarch's nephews and nieces rank immediately behind their parents according to gender and birth-order bias.

Objective

Students assemble a genealogical chart and apply monarchial succession rules.

Task

Students sort and order birth, marriage, and death dates to create a genealogical chart for a fictional royal family, and learn rules of British monarchial succession to identify those eligible for the throne in the order of precedence.

Input

For King Richard IV's succession in 1725, the order of precedence from first to last was Charles, Andrew, William, Walter, Catherine, Helen, John, Oliver, and Henry. Prince Charles will be the next monarch in this fictional line of British royalty.

Metacognitive Discussion

How did you organize the information to build the chart accurately? How else can you use a chart showing biological relationships?

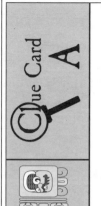

Clue Card A

1. Richard had two sons, Prince Charles and Prince Andrew, by his wife, the former Alexandra Hughes.
2. Mary's first two sons were born 20 months apart.
3. Richard IV became king in 1725.
4. Establish the years of birth for every member of the family.
5. Richard's second son was born two years after the first, arriving on Richard's 27th birthday.
6. William had three offspring—Catherine, Helen, and Walter. William's wife was Susan Spencer.

Clue Card B

1. Andrew was 12 years old when his father became king but died of an illness less than a year after the succession.
2. Richard was the eldest son born to James V and Mary. He was two years older than the second-born.
3. Ania was the third child born to James and Mary.
4. John was 10 years old when his sister died. Mary died at age 59.
5. Walter, who was three years older than his baby sister, was eight years old when his grandfather died.
6. Andrew was the youngest child.
7. The Duchess of Saxony was born Gwendolyn Armstrong in 1672.

Clue Card C

1. John, the Duke of Gloucester, was Richard's younger brother. James V died at age 60.
2. Ania (whose mother was also named Mary) had two sons born only slightly more than a year apart. One was Henry, His Grace the Duke of Wales, and the other was Oliver, the Duke of Hanover.
3. Walter was older than Helen. Anna and William were born two years apart.
4. The Duke of Saxony had two sons, Philip and Patrick. Philip was first born.
5. Each child ranks immediately behind his or her parent according to the prevailing gender and birth order bias.
6. Catherine and Andrew were born in the same year.

Clue Card D

1. Robert's sons were one year younger and one year older than Richard.
2. Ania died in 1720. She was 30 years of age at the time of her death.
3. The elder son was Oliver, who was the same age as the Duke of Gloucester.
4. Ania had two older brothers, one of whom was named William.
5. James had a younger brother by three years, Robert, the Duke of Saxony.
6. Walter was the middle child. Ania married Terrence Whitfield at age 18.

SkyLight Training and Publishing Inc.

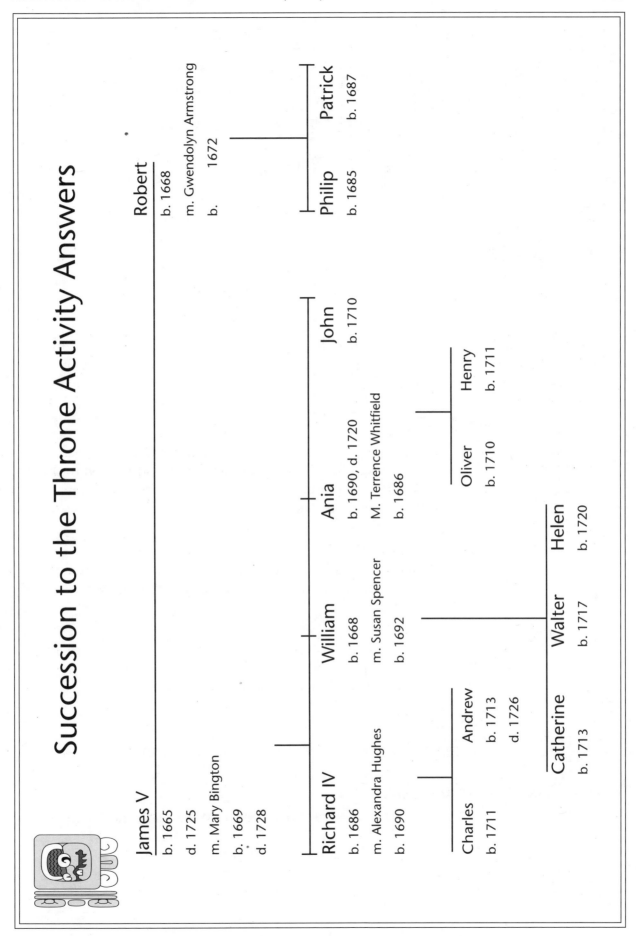

Succession to the Throne Activity Answers

James V
b. 1665
d. 1725
m. Mary Bington
b. 1669
d. 1728

Robert
b. 1668
m. Gwendolyn Armstrong
b.   1672

Philip
b. 1685

Patrick
b. 1687

John
b. 1710

Ania
b. 1690, d. 1720
M. Terrence Whitfield
b. 1686

Oliver
b. 1710

Henry
b. 1711

Richard IV
b. 1686
m. Alexandra Hughes
b. 1690

William
b. 1668
m. Susan Spencer
b. 1692

Walter
b. 1717

Helen
b. 1720

Charles
b. 1711

Andrew
b. 1713
d. 1726

Catherine
b. 1713

Succession to the British Throne (Part 2)

Activity 28

Students update the genealogical chart they constructed for a fictional royal family in "Succession to the British Throne (Part 1)" and name the suspect in an attempted assassination.

Background Information

Teachers may wish to remind students of succession rules given in the Background Information section of "Succession to the British Throne (Part 1)." To eliminate guessing, each team should be allowed only two chances to name their suspect.

Objective

Students increase their understanding of genealogical charting methodology and succession in a hereditary monarchy.

Task

Students deduce a motive for an attempted assassination after updating a genealogical chart they created and by applying the rules of British monarchial succession.

Input

Prince John, who wants to be king, is the suspect.

Metacognitive Discussion

How did you arrive at the answer? What other methods can you use to discover reasons for another person's actions? How can you apply them in reading literature and history?

Clue Card A

1. Since mid-January, King Richard has been suffering from ill health. It is just a matter of time before he expires.
2. The wife of Prince William's son is titled the Duchess of Kent.
3. In early March, John and his bride, Princess Lydia, depart for a holiday in Scotland.
4. In late February in France, the Duke of Hanover suffers a concussion after he suffered a nasty fall from his horse as it went over the first jump. The saddle cinches appear to have been cut.
5. Princess Catherine dies of consumption in 1726.

Clue Card B

1. Scotland Yard believes there is a plot to alter the order of royal succession.
2. The armed escort foils the deadly attack by outlaws on Prince Charles's caravan.
3. Name the prime suspect and identify the motive in the murder plot!
4. The French would like nothing more than to see the Britons in political chaos.
5. Prince William dies in his sleep in early April.

Clue Card C

1. The Duke of Wales's brother is named Oliver.
2. The food taster at the table of the Queen and Prince Charles dies from either a heart attack or poison.
3. Members of the British royal family are hated by the Scots and the Irish.
4. Princess Helen is killed in a riding accident in 1728.
5. The dukedom (or duchy) of Saxony is vacant as all heirs have been deceased for five years.

Clue Card D

1. At a fox hunt, a sniper wounds the Duke of Kent with an arrow.
2. Prince John sends word that suggests that security should be stepped up for King Richard.
3. The younger son of Ania could not be warned of the danger at home. He has joined an order of monks (who have taken an oath of silence) on the continent over two years ago.
4. Use the genealogical chart you established in the "Succession to the British Throne (Part 1)" activity.

Royal Surfing (Part 1)

Activity 29

Note: Access to the World Wide Web (the Internet) will be necessary for this activity.

Students search the Internet (surf the Net) to learn about the Belgian royal dynasty and order of succession.

Background Information

Students must be familiar with using the Internet and its search engines. Teachers may wish to refer to the first two paragraphs under Background Information for "Succession to the British Throne (Part 1)" for information on a genealogical chart.

Objective

Students increase their familiarity with Internet search engines, draw a genealogical chart, and apply rules of cognatic monarchial succession.

Task

Students employ Internet search engines to identify a country, research and draw a genealogical chart, and determine the order of succession in Belgium.

Input

Following are the answers to the activity: A4, Albert I, Elizabeth; B3, Laurent; C3, Leopold III, Astrid; D1, Donna Paola; D2, Astrid; D4, Phillippe.

Metacognitive Discussion

How did you find the information for the chart? How will you use an Internet search engine more effectively in the future?

Clue Card A

1. Like most of the other European countries with constitutional monarchies, this country uses a cognatic order of succession.
2. The government of this country is located in the city of Brussels.
3. Most monarchies previously used agnatic succession, whereby the crown was passed only to the males of the family.
4. Who were Leopold III's parents?

Clue Card B

1. Construct the genealogical chart from Albert I to the current heirs to the throne.
2. Albert II was not the crown prince.
3. If this country were still using the agnatic rules for succession, name the person who would be next in line for the throne after the current heir.
4. Albert's two grandsons were born four years apart.

Clue Card C

1. The elder grandson, named Baudouin, was born in 1930.
2. Use the Internet to find the information you need.
3. Who were Albert II's father and mother?
4. The title of Crown Prince or Crown Princess is given to that member of the royal family who is the immediate heir to the throne according to succession rules.
5. Albert II was named after his grandfather.

Clue Card D

1. Who married Albert II?
2. If the member of the royal family born in 1960 dies, who is the next heir to the throne?
3. This country is found on the European continent.
4. Who is the current heir to the throne?
5. In a cognatic succession, the throne goes to the monarch's eldest child—male or female—when succession is in order.

SkyLight Training and Publishing Inc.

Royal Surfing (Part 2)

Activity 30

Note: Access to the World Wide Web (the Internet) will be necessary for this activity.

Students learn about Norway's royal family and order of succession by searching the Internet.

Background Information

Students must be familiar with using the Internet and its search engines. Teachers may wish to refer to the first two paragraphs under Background Information for "Succession to the British Throne (Part I)" for the purpose of and information on a genealogical chart.

Objective

Students increase their familiarity with Internet search engines, draw a genealogical chart, and apply rules of monarchial succession.

Task

Students use Internet information to identify Norway, assemble a genealogical chart of its royal family, and explain the order of succession for its current heirs.

Input

Prince Haakon is the current heir rather than his elder sister because agnatic succession applies to children born before 1990.

Metacognitive Discussion

How did you find the answers? How will you use an Internet search engine more effectively in the future?

SkyLight Training and Publishing Inc.

Clue Card A

1. In 1996, King Harald's son came to the United States to study political science.
2. The capital city of this Scandinavian country is not Stockholm.
3. In 1905, this country dissolved its union with another country.
4. One king was named Olav.

Clue Card B

1. Queen Sonja's two children attended local primary and secondary schools.
2. To marry a person born outside royal heritage is to marry a "commoner."
3. This country seceded from another in 1814.
4. Construct the royal genealogical chart for this Scandinavian country. Show all four generations.

Clue Card C

1. The title Crown Prince or Crown Princess is given to that member of the royal family who is the immediate heir to the throne according to succession rules.
2. Use the Internet to find the information you need.
3. This country approved first agnatic and then cognatic succession.
4. In 1928, Olav won an Olympic gold medal for this country in sailing.

Clue Card D

1. After the dissolution, a prince of another country became this country's king.
2. Name the current heir to the throne.
3. The capital city of this Scandinavian country is not Helsinki.
4. King Haakon VII was born in 1872.
5. King Harald was the first prince born in this country in 567 years.

SkyLight Training and Publishing Inc.

Roman Numerals

Activity 31

Students learn or reinforce their knowledge of Roman numerals.

Objective

Students become proficient in a new counting system that uses seven symbols, does not have a zero, and orders numbers horizontally from both left and right.

Task

Students deduce and name the values of the seven symbols of the Roman numeral system.

Metacognitive Discussion

Is it difficult to remember when you are supposed to add to or subtract from an adjacent number? How do you differentiate? In what other circumstances do you use this sort of process to understand things?

1. By placing a bar over the top of a Roman numeral, you multiply the value of that symbol by 1,000.
2. CM = 1,000 - 100
3. If a symbol of lesser value immediately follows a greater symbol, it is added to the symbol.
4. Roman numerals are formed by the principle of addition from left to right; however, for numbers having values of 4 and 9, the principle of subtraction is used. For example, IV = 4, IX =9, XL = 40, and XC = 90.

1. If a symbol of lesser value immediately precedes a greater symbol, it is subtracted from the symbol.
2. DC - CD = CC
3. V + I = X - IV
4. In the Roman system, when you have a choice, write the number in the way that uses the fewest symbols.
5. CC = (C + L + XXV + XVIII + VII)

1. Roman numerals are often used in outlines, chapter titles, parts of books, and at the end of credits for television programs and films—to indicate copyright year.
2. Roman numerals use seven core symbols for their computations.
3. XXX + XXX = LX, or 60
4. XXV = 25,000
5. MC = 1,000 + 100 and CM = 1,000 - 100
6. V = 5,000

1. When working with Roman numerals, it's important to note whether a symbol of lesser value precedes or follows a symbol of greater value.
2. MCMXC = 1,990
3. What are the seven symbols of the Roman numeral system and what are the values of each?
4. 2,000,000 - 1,000,000 = M

Mayan Math (Part 1)

Activity 32

Students learn the ancient Mayan counting system, which used vertical stacking, three symbols, a base of 20, and zero.

Background Information

It may be helpful to assign the "Roman Numerals" activity first so students can practice lining up nonarabic symbols horizontally; with the Mayan counting system, they will learn to stack three symbols vertically.

Teachers may wish to show photos of art and architecture of the Mayan Classic Era as they give the following information to students:

The ancient Maya were a group of Indian peoples who lived in southern Mexico as well as in Guatemala, Honduras, and Belize. The Mayan and Aztecan cultures are known as Middle American, or Meso-American, civilizations.

Archaeologists have discovered the ruins of the Mayan Classic Era. The civilization flourished until about 1,100 years ago, at which time it suddenly vanished. No historian or archaeologist has ever been able to explain why or how these people disappeared. Their descendants are found in Central America today, but the Classic Era mysteriously disappeared.

The Classic Era Maya were the first people of the New World known to keep historical records. Because little evidence of warfare has been recognized archaeologically, they were thought to be peaceful timekeepers and sky watchers, although they did practice human torture and sacrifice.

Mathematics, calendars, and astronomy were important to the

SkyLight Training and Publishing Inc.

Mesoamerican cultures, especially the Mayan. In order to study these areas, the Maya developed an interesting and accurate system of counting and calculating. Mayan math is based on the number 20. This system is called a vigesimal system. It has been speculated that the vigesimal system probably stemmed from people using both their toes and their fingers to calculate.

Objective

Students learn a counting system that uses vertical stacking, three symbols, a base of 20, and zero.

Task

Students demonstrate an understanding of Mayan math.

Input

Students deduce the two missing symbols and their values as follows: a ●[dot] = 1 and a ▬▬▬▬[bar] = 5.

Metacognitive Discussion

How did you figure out the missing symbols and their values? How will you more quickly figure out other symbols' meanings in other courses in the future?

SkyLight Training and Publishing Inc.

Clue Card A

1. The Maya were one of the first of the few civilizations to use the concept of zero in their numbering and computations.
2. A place in the Mayan counting system can hold up to 19 characters.
3. What are the values of the two remaining symbols of the Mayan counting system?

Clue Card B

1. Mayan numbers were written in vertical columns, with the lowest value place at the bottom for 1 through 19.
2. A rule of the Mayan numbering system is never to use four bars in a single value place location; use a dot on a higher level instead.
3. Remember that in the Arabic numeral system, the lowest number is placed to the right.

Clue Card C

1. In the Arabic numeral system, numbers are written horizontally from right to left.
2. What are the values of the two remaining symbols of Mayan math?
3. A rule of Mayan numbering is to not use five dots on the same level in a number.

Clue Card D

1. Mayan numbers are stacked as high as necessary. The greater the number, the higher the stack will be.
2. The Maya used only three written digits, or symbols, for their numbering system.
3. The digit/symbol for zero in the Mayan numbering system looked like a shell.

SkyLight Training and Publishing Inc.

Mayan Math (Part 2)

Activity 33

Students increase their understanding of the Mayan counting system rules by completing a table and a chart.

Background Information

Teachers need to assign this activity only after students understand the Mayan counting system rules given in "Mayan Math (Part 1)" and before they attempt "Search for the Zytar (Part 3)," which gives students more practice in it.

It might be necessary to demonstrate how Mayan figures are written.

Objective

Students apply Mayan counting system rules to become proficient in the system.

Task

Students translate Arabic numbers into Mayan numbers to complete a table and a chart.

Input

Refer to figures 4.2–4.5.

Metacognitive Discussion

How are Mayan numbers like Arabic numbers? Roman numerals? How is the Mayan system different from Arbaic? Roman? How does understanding the Mayan system help you to understand mathematics better?

Clue Card A

1. The Maya were one of the first of the few civilizations to use the concept of zero in their numbering and computations.
2. A place value in the Mayan counting system can hold up to 19 characters.
3. Depict values using all 19 characters.
4. In the 20s column, the characters totaling 13 are the same as saying 13 x 20.

Clue Card B

1. Mayan numbers were written in vertical columns, with the lowest value place at the bottom for 1 through 19.
2. A rule of the Mayan numbering system is never to use four bars; use a dot instead.
3. Depict values using all 19 characters.
4. Remember that in the decimal system the lowest number is placed to the right.
5. Mayan numbers with zero in them that can be divided evenly by the number 20 will have at least 1 ⬭ in their depiction.

Clue Card C

1. In the Arabic numeral system, the numbers are written horizontally from right to left.
2. Fill in the chart translating the Arabic numbers into Mayan numbers.
3. The Maya used a number system based on the number 20.
4. A rule of Mayan numbering is never to use five dots in a number.

Clue Card D

1. Mayan numbers are stacked as high as necessary. The greater the number, the higher the stack will be.
2. The Maya used only three written digits or symbols for their numbering system.
3. The digit/symbol for zero in Mayan numbers looked like ⬭.
4. Fill in the table depicting the Mayan counting system through the first four places.
5. In the Mayan vertical vigesimal system, the ones place is always the bottom symbol. On top of it is the twenties place, on top of the twenties place is the four hundreds place, and so on.

SkyLight Training and Publishing Inc.

Mayan Math Activity (Part 2): Chart 1

• 1	⊂⊃ 20	400	8,000
• • 2	⊂⊃ 40	800	16,000
• • • 3	⊂⊃ 60	1,200	24,000
• • • • 4	⊂⊃ 80	1,600	32,000
▬ 5	⊂⊃ 100	2,000	40,000
▬ • 6	⊂⊃ 120	2,400	48,000
▬ • • 7	⊂⊃ 140	2,800	56,000
▬ • • • 8	⊂⊃ 160	3,200	64,000
▬ • • • • 9	⊂⊃ 180	3,600	72,000
▬▬ 10	⊂⊃ 200	4,000	80,000
▬▬ • 11	⊂⊃ 220	4,400	88,000
▬▬ • • 12	⊂⊃ 240	4,800	96,000
▬▬ • • • 13	⊂⊃ 260	5,200	104,000
▬▬ • • • • 14	⊂⊃ 280	5,600	112,000
▬▬▬ 15	⊂⊃ 300	6,000	120,000
▬▬▬ • 16	⊂⊃ 320	6,400	128,000
▬▬▬ • • 17	⊂⊃ 340	6,800	136,000
▬▬▬ • • • 18	⊂⊃ 360	7,200	144,000
▬▬▬ • • • • 19	⊂⊃ 380	7,600	152,000

Mayan Math (Part 2): Chart 1 Worksheet

•	1	⬭	20	⬭	400	⬭	8,000
• •	2	⬭	40	⬭	800	⬭	16,000
• • •	3	⬭	60	⬭	1,200	⬭	24,000
• • • •	4	⬭	80		1,600	⬭	32,000
▬	5	⬭					
▬ •	6	⬭					
▬ • •	7	⬭					
▬ • • •	8	⬭					
▬ • • • •	9	⬭					
▬▬	10	⬭					
▬▬ •	11		220				
▬▬ • •	12						
▬▬ • • •	13						
▬▬ • • • •	14						
▬▬▬	15		300	⬭	6,000		
▬▬▬ •	16						
▬▬▬ • •	17						
▬▬▬ • • •	18						
▬▬▬ • • • •	19	⬭					152,000
⬭	20	⬭		⬭	8,000		

Figure 4.3

SkyLight Training and Publishing Inc.

Mayan Math Activity (Part 2):
Chart 2

21	381	8,409
37	277	25,662
53	421	731
62	399	169
75	213	8,106
214	1,285	501
126	30	1,997
406	16,842	4,205

Mayan Math (Part 2):
Chart 2 Worksheet

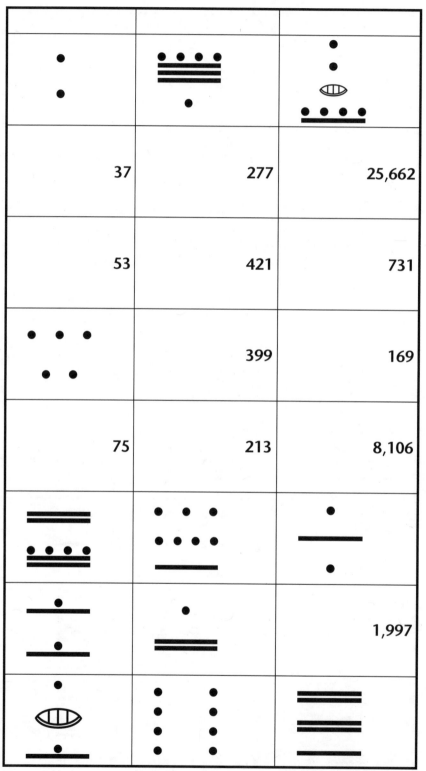

Note: In this activity the student either gives the Arabic numeral equal to the Mayan symbol, or vice versa.

Figure 4.5

SkyLight Training and Publishing Inc.

Search for the Zytar (Part 1)

Activity 34

Students learn about Mayan, Incan, and Aztecan culture, history, government, and geography by conducting a search for a fictional object, a Zytar.

Background Information

To prepare the teams, teachers may employ the jigsaw strategy, whereby all students drawing A cards huddle to review their information, and students drawing B, C, and D cards respectively do the same, before regrouping in the usual A-B-C-D team structure.

Teams have only two opportunities to check their answers with the teacher; any more chances allow them simply to guess. When checking a team's answers, the teacher should not comment on which of the three are correct; otherwise, the students arrive at the other two answers through elimination and not by further discussing and absorbing the information.

Relay the following information to the students, setting the stage for the activity. Of course, the story line is fictional; however, the information about the early Central American and South American Indian civilizations is true.

Three archaeologists recently discovered and tried to translate an amazing document about an object called the Zytar. The document seemed to reveal that the Zytar was left by extraterrestrials who visited the Indians of Mesoamerica and the Andean terrain. If their translation is correct, the Zytar holds great power and knowledge. According to a legend, the extraterrestrials left the scepter-like object behind for humans to use when they were ready to advance their civilizations.

The three archaeologists have a hunch the Zytar is somewhere in Central or South America. To them, the idea of the human race advancing is hogwash. They intend to find the Zytar and sell it to the dictator willing to pay the highest price. They immediately travel in secret to three different locations to dig for the Zytar.

You are one of the extraterrestrials who hid the Zytar on the planet Earth a long time ago. You did this because of your great love for the human race. Even with all the things the humans do wrong so much of the time, you see all the love in their hearts and all the ways they try to do things right. You will be happy once the earthlings finally are wise enough to use the powerful gift you hid for them. Far away from Earth, you monitor your hiding place to keep it safe. The time will come when the humans can use it, but you know they are not yet ready for it now.

You are horrified that three archaeologists are hunting for the Zytar so they can sell it to one of the worst kinds of earthlings. They're so far from finding it that you know they never will, but you're worried they'll start babbling about the Zytar to other greedy people. And besides, people with names like Icame, Isaw, and Iconquered probably don't know much about peace, do they?

Your plan is to figure out exactly where the three archaeologists are and beam a special kind of mind-altering ray at them. They'll forget all about the Zytar's existence and their evil scheme. They will go back to doing the kind of work archaeologists should do. They will change their names to Faith, Hope, and Charity and, one day, they will write a wonderful book about the Aztecan, Incan, and Mayan cultures.

Your task right now is to pick up their radio transmissions and determine which archaeologist is at which site. Later, you can set up the ray.

Radio Transmission of Archaeologists Icame, Isaw, and Iconquered:

Iconquered: Hello, Icame! Have you had any luck in determining if the object might be located at your site?

Icame: No, Iconquered, it is too early to tell. How about you, Isaw?

Isaw: No luck either. I am going over the artifacts trying to learn about these people.

Icame: All of the sand around here has made my maps useless!

Iconquered: Icame, you may have to move soon to your alternate site. If you don't move in the next four weeks, the frigid weather at your altitude will make a dig impossible.

Icame: I found what looks to be a Spanish helmet.

Isaw: I have found a great many swords and helmets.

Iconquered: I have not found any of those yet.

Isaw: On the wall of a temple here, I found a drawing of the sun.

Icame: I, too, have seen drawings of the sun!

Iconquered: Isaw, I have discovered drawings and what looks to be charts of stars and constellations.

Isaw: There are also extensive drawings of the stars at night at my site.

Icame: I keep finding wagons and horseshoes.

Isaw: By the number of skulls I found around the temple, they must have practiced a lot of sacrifices.

Iconquered: The drawings on the walls of my temple show that the people have needle-like objects in their ears.

Objective

Students learn about the culture, history, government, and geography of early Central American and South American Indian civilizations.

Task

Students match the archaeologist with the civilization site.

Input

Icame—Incan, Isaw—Aztecan, and Iconquered—Mayan.

Metacognitive Discussion

How did you figure out which archaeologist was at which site? How can you conduct the same kind of process more accurately the next time?

Clue Card A

1. The state religion of the Inca centered on the worship of the sun.
2. Approximately 20,000 kilometers (12,000 miles) of Incan roads constituted a transportation network rivaled only by that of the Romans in the pre-industrial world.
3. Aztecs occupied the Valley of Mexico from 1200 to 1521.
4. Irrigation systems were especially important in the coastal desert regions of the Incan empire. Most of the systems there were built long before the Inca conquered the region.
5. The Aztecs' conquests furnished war captives for their many sacrifices to the gods.
6. At the time of its demise, the Incan empire controlled an estimated 12 million people in much of what is now Peru and Ecuador, as well as large areas of Chile, Bolivia, and Argentina.
7. The Maya were the first people of the New World to keep historical records. They also made significant advances in mathematics, astronomy, architecture, and calendar making.
8. The Aztecan priests were expected to live in chastity; to mortify their flesh; and to understand astronomy, astrology, complex religious rituals and ceremonies, and the art of picture writing.
9. Two so-called "royal roads" were built so Incan rulers could travel the length of the empire. One road was near the coast and one was through the Andean highland.

Clue Card B

1. The Aztecs were famous warriors with a highly developed military system.
2. The Inca called their land *Tawantinsuyu,* which means "four parts." They lived in a land of markedly diverse terrain and climate. Their land included desert, valleys, mountains, and the tropical forest to the east.
3. The Maya's Classic Era is believed to have occurred from 250 to 900 A.D.
4. The average Aztecan Indian was probably a farmer.
5. With the arrival in 1519 of the Spanish army of Hernán Cortés, several Mexican cities willingly joined forces with the invaders to overthrow the Aztecs.
6. The Inca were the rulers of the largest native empire of the Americas.
7. Because little evidence of warfare had been recognized archaeologically, the Maya of the Classic Era were thought of as peaceful timekeepers and sky watchers.
8. Montezuma I expanded the Aztecan empire until it stretched from the Atlantic to the Pacific coasts. A total of 489 cities paid tribute to the alliance.
9. The Incan emperors were believed to be descended from the sun god and were worshiped as divine beings.
10. Incan religious practices included consulting oracles, offering sacrifices, religious trances, and public confessions.
11. The cultures of the Maya and the Aztecs are known as Middle American, or Mesoamerican, civilizations.

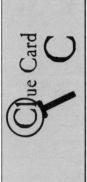

1. The agricultural year and the annual cycle of religious festivals were regulated by the extremely accurate Incan calendar.
2. The Aztecs' religious practices included large-scale human sacrifice.
3. Expansion was achieved in part as the result of a program of brutal invasions and conquests by the Incan armies. The expansion ended with the Spanish invasion.
4. The ancient Maya were a group of Indian peoples who lived in southern Mexico as well as in Guatemala, Honduras, and Belize.
5. Gold, the symbol of the sun god, was mined extensively for use by the Incan rulers and members of the elite, not as a means of exchange but principally for decorative and ritualistic purposes.
6. Schooling and training in the martial arts were compulsory for all Aztecan boys.
7. Religion was in the hands of full-time priests, whose leaders were drawn from the Aztecan ruling families; thus, no conflict of interest existed between church and state.
8. An unusual characteristic of the Incan state was internal colonization, the ability to move people and to place loyal groups in regions that were difficult to control.
9. Because of civil war in the Incan state, the Spaniards were able to take the Incan ruler captive and cause empire's collapse.

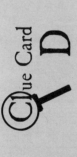

1. The Aztecs had large cities controlled by well-organized governments.
2. Maize and beans formed the Mayan diet then as today, although squash, tomatoes, peppers, fruits, and game also were consumed.
3. Near the end of the fourteenth century, the Incan empire began to expand in the Andean Mountains of South America. Less than two centuries later, the empire fell abruptly with the Spanish invasion led by Francisco Pizarro in 1532.
4. The Maya practiced human torture and sacrifice. Blood was the major offering to their gods. Male nobles drew blood from their ear or tongue, and female nobles drew blood from the tongue. Priests drew blood from the ears, fingers, and mouths of war captives before they were sacrificed.
5. The Aztecs considered themselves the chosen people of the sun and war god, in whose name they were destined to conquer all rival nations.
6. The term *Inca* refers to the ruler himself as well as to the people.
7. From these conquered cities came foodstuffs and exotic raw materials lacking in the Aztecan homeland—gold, copper, tropical feathers, gemstones, rubber, jade, amber, jaguar skins, and chocolate.
8. The Maya were never really united into a political empire; instead, they lived in city-states much like those of ancient Greece.
9. The Incan state was not a monolith under the absolute control of its ruler.
10. The empire was held together by force rather than by loyalty, and the subject states were eager to shake off Aztecan control.

SkyLight Training and Publishing Inc.

Search for the Zytar (Part 2)

Activity 35

Students deduce the identity of a civilization and answer questions about it.

Background Information

Before presenting the new information below, redistribute the clue cards from "Search for the Zytar (Part 1)."

To prepare the teams, teachers again may employ the jigsaw strategy, whereby all students drawing A cards gather to review their information, and students drawing B, C, and D cards respectively do the same, before students regroup in the usual A-B-C-D team structure.

The teacher should grade all five answers as one, but not comment on individual answers; otherwise, the students can guess the answers through elimination. If students are correct on all five answers, the teacher only should acknowledge that the task is completed for that team.

Teachers may elect to tell students to pay attention to clues about terrain and climate.

Relay the following information to the students, setting the stage for this activity. The story line about the extraterrestrials and the Zytar, of course, is fictional; however, the information about the Mesoamericans is true.

As the extraterrestrial guarding the Zytar, you plan to keep the three archaeologists from breaking the secret of its existence. You become alarmed when you pick up a radio transmission. You know none of them possibly can find it—they are much

SkyLight Training and Publishing Inc.

too far away from it. Yet, suddenly, one of them seems to have found another document and is asking the other two to come quickly to examine it. All you can hear is the following:

"... I have found travel overland to the different cities here very, very difficult. The jungles are tough—it was probably this way when the civilization flourished. If you travel by boat, you can reach either coast quickly ..."

Your task is to discover where the new document is so you can get the mind-altering ray set up to zap all three quickly. First, answer the following questions about which civilization had the secret document. Soon all three archaeologists will be at that site. You must get all of the answers correct to aim the ray correctly and save the secret of the Zytar.

1. Which archaeologist radioed the other two? Was it Icame, Isaw, or Iconquered?

2. Which Indian civilization might have had the new document about the Zytar? Was it the Mayan, the Incan, or the Aztecan?

3. When did the civilization exist?
   - 1200–1251 A.D.?
   - 250–900 A.D.?
   - 1300–1532 A.D.?

4. Did the Spanish bring about the collapse of this particular civilization?

5. Was this a tightly or loosely organized political society?

Objective

Students sharpen their attention to detail in problem-solving.

Task

Students identify a civilization and answer questions about it.

Input

Iconquered radioed the other two to come to the site of the Mayan Classic Era civilization, which existed from 250 to 900 A.D. The Spanish did not cause the collapse of this loosely organized political society.

Metacognitive Discussion

How did you find the answer?

SkyLight Training and Publishing Inc.

Search for the Zytar (Part 3)

Activity 36

Students deduce the code using their knowledge of the Mayan counting system to translate a message first into Arabic numbers and then into our alphabet.

Background Information

Students should successfully complete "Mayan Math (Part 2)" before attempting this activity. The story line about the Zytar is fictional, but the Maya did use the numbers and symbols shown in the chart below.

Teachers may suggest to students having difficulty with the activity to begin by writing out the alphabet from A to Z as a graphic organizer (see page 171).

Objective

Students increase their competence in working with another counting system and use problem-solving and analytical skills to decipher a code.

Task

Students deduce the code using their knowledge of the Mayan counting system to translate a message first into Arabic numbers and then into our alphabet.

SkyLight Training and Publishing Inc.

Input

See figure 4.6 (Search for the Zytar [Part 3]: Message on the Wall) as reference.

- **F**orward 20 paces from temple
- First step turn to sunrise
- Step 50 paces
- Gold in tomb 10 feet below surface

Students break the code as follows: First write out our alphabet in one straight line. Then apply the numbers in the following fashion, as stated in the clues:

A B C D E F G H I J K L M N O P Q R S T U V W X Y Z
14 15 16 17 18 19 20 21 22 23 24 25 26 13 12 11 10 9 8 7 6 5 4 3 2 1

Clues A4, A2, B2, C1, D1, and D3 indicate this process.

Students first translate the Mayan numeral into an Arabic numeral and then substitute a letter with the matching translated numeral according to the code. For example, the Mayan symbol ▬▬▬ = 19, which by use of the code translates into the letter "**F**."

Metacognitive Discussion

How did you decipher the code?

1. You must decipher the inscription on the Mayan temple wall and translate it into English.
2. In this coded message, ▭ is the Mayan symbol for Q.
3. You believe that the numbers stand for letters in this coded message.
4. For this coded message, the Maya used 26 letters in their alphabet.

1. In this coded message, numbers are numbers!
2. In this coded message, the letter A is the Arabic number 14 as well as the Mayan number 14.
3. Glyphs are picture symbols.

1. In this coded message, ● is the Mayan symbol used for the letter Z.
2. The Mayan writing system used glyphs.
3. Egyptian writing was known as hieroglyphics.

1. In this coded message, 17 is the Arabic number for the letter D.
2. Translate the message into English.
3. The word *rate* is written using the Arabic symbols 9 14 7 18 in this coded message.

Search for the Zytar (Part 3)
Message on the Wall

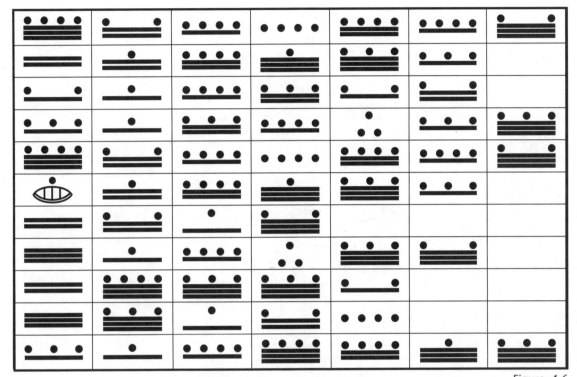

Figure 4.6

Decoded Message

19	12	9	4	14	9	17
10	11	14	16	18	8	
7	6	9	13	7	12	
8	6	13	9	22	8	18
19	12	9	4	14	9	17
20	11	14	16	18	8	
10	12	25	17			
15	6	9	22	18	17	
10	19	18	18	7		
15	18	25	12	4		
8	6	9	19	14	16	18

Figure 4.7

History

Perspectives on Past Events

History:

Perspectives on Past Events

American history, government, economics, and business teachers can use Part V activities either to supplement specific topics or assist in the year-end review.

To supplement their coverage of different eras, American history teachers may assign "The American Revolution," "The 1850s," and "The Roaring Twenties." Each activity requires students to sort through the data and unravel the information, just as historians do, to create a time line.

Government, math, and American history students count up Electoral College votes in "The Election of 1824," the one presidential election in our history that was decided by the House of Representatives. Teachers can elect to use it with Part II's "The Electoral College and the Election of 1824," "Apportionment," and "Apportionment: The Equal Proportions Method."

American history teachers may find the last two activities in this part especially helpful for year-end reviews.

For the "What's in a Name?" activity, students match every president with his nickname or indicate that he did not have one. The nicknames make interesting material for discussion. Are they simplistic or deft characterizations of the presidents' terms in office, contributions to public life or personal modes of operating? At what point does a clever mnemonic device stop being clever and start being glib?

"Five Great Presidents" derives from the results of a 1995 survey of 168 historians on the historical ranking of American presidents. This activity focuses on those who emerged as the five top-rated presidents; they may be the favorites of the students, too.

The American Revolution

Activity 37

Students increase their understanding of the reasons behind the American Revolution.

Objective

Students understand the reasons for the American Revolution.

Task

Students correctly order 15 events to create a time line.

Input

Proclamation of 1763; Sugar Act–1964; Stamp Act–1765; Stamp Act Congress–1765; Repeal of the Stamp Act–1766; Townshend Acts–1767; Boston Massacre–March 5, 1770; Committees of Correspondence–1772; Tea Act–1773; Boston Tea Party–December 16, 1773; Intolerable Acts–1774; First Continental Congress–September and October, 1774; Lexington and Concord–April 18, 1775; Second Continental Congress begins–May 10, 1775; Declaration of Independence–July 1776.

Metacognitive Discussion

When you began this activity, were you aware that you had never experienced the thinking and the information required to complete this activity? Could you now handle a similar activity for a different era with different information? In the future what information will you know to look for, and how will you begin looking for it? The next time you do a similar activity, what will you do so you can complete it more quickly than you did this one?

SkyLight Training and Publishing Inc.

1. One month before the third meeting of the colonies, fighting between the colonists and the British occurred in two Massachusetts towns.
2. In the same year, following the acts of British reprisal, the colonists called for their second meeting of the colonies. Representatives of 12 of the 13 colonies attended, and they agreed to meet for a third time a year later.
3. This Proclamation line was drawn to keep colonial settlers safe from Indian attack and to keep settlements and farms from eating up newly won French territory that was rich in furs.
4. Under a new prime minister, Parliament levied a fourth British tax six years after its last taxation legislation. Parliament passed the tax to help the British East India Company prevail over its Dutch rival. The tax prompted a "celebration" of sorts later that year.
5. Victory in the New World's 1756–1763 French and Indian War (known in Europe as the Seven Years' War) brought mixed results for Great Britain.

1. Parliament passed the first tax legislation affecting the colonists. The tax was on molasses and other sweet goods imported to the colonies. It would be a full decade before 12 out of 13 colonies would meet in Philadelphia to discuss British actions.
2. The British had control over much of North America, but the war erased all profits the British had ever collected from owning the colonies.
3. After the riot, it was agreed that the colonists would keep up with British activity by forming communication groups. Samuel Adams is credited with assembling the first meeting, which was held in 1772, in which 80 Massachusetts towns participated.
4. The second tax, passed the next year at Prime Minister Grenville's urging, placed an internal tax on the colonists; that is, it would be collected within the colonies. Any legal document, such as a will, license, or a deed, would need one of these.
5. Only in three years—1768, 1769, and 1771—was there not any official move or event recorded that resulted in greater difficulties between Great Britian and the colonies.

1. To make sure the colonists had no more "celebrations" like the last one, the British tightened the reins the next year with further legislation. The British officially called them the "Repressive Acts," but the colonists chose to call them by another descriptive name.
2. Its national debt more than doubled because of the war, and Great Britain had the added burden of keeping troops in the New World to protect the empire's gains.
3. Almost fifteen months after the fighting broke out, the colonists changed their reasons for fighting the British when this document was approved.
4. List these following events on a time line: the Boston Massacre, Boston Tea Party, Committees of Correspondence, Declaration of Independence, First Continental Congress, Intolerable Acts, Lexington and Concord, Repeal of the Stamp Act, Second Continental Congress begins, Sugar Act, Stamp Act, Stamp Act Congress, Tea Act, and Townshend Acts.

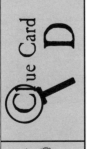

1. Still determined to raise revenue, and assert its right to tax the colonists, the British government made a third attempt to levy taxes on the colonists. This taxation bore the name of Great Britian's new prime minister.
2. Three years after the third tax was passed, a riot broke out, and British soldiers inflicted causalities in this northern colonial city.
3. The same year that the war ended, the British began this series of events by drawing a line and forbidding the colonists to cross it.
4. Parliament raised taxes to an all-time high. Prime Minister George Grenville eyed the American colonies as a new source of tax revenue.
5. Boycotts of British goods, the formation of the Sons of Liberty, and a meeting of delegates from nine colonies resulted from anger over the second British tax.

THE ELECTION OF 1824

Activity 38

Students learn how the Electoral College cast its votes in the only presidential election decided by the House of Representatives.

Background Information

In 1824, four equally strong candidates ran for president. Each did well in the general election—so well that the Electoral College could not declare a winner. Senator Andrew Jackson of Tennessee emerged from the pack with a plurality of votes but not a majority. According to the Constitution, a candidate must receive a majority of the electoral votes. But if no one does, the election of the president then is decided by a vote in the House of Representatives.

After a disabling stroke, William Crawford of Virginia was dropped from the ranks of serious contenders. Henry Clay, although polling more popular votes than Crawford, was eliminated because, according to the Constitution, only the top three candidates in an undecided electoral race can be considered in the vote in the House of Representatives. But Clay, a Kentuckian, was not through. He held the powerful position of Speaker of the House, and he used his influence to play a major role in deciding who would be the next president. Clay met with John Quincy Adams.

Adams, Massachusetts' favorite son, emerged the winner. Adams received votes in the House election from states that had not given him electoral votes. Andrew Jackson was incensed.

SkyLight Training and Publishing Inc.

Objective

Students calculate the number of each state's electoral votes and how the votes were distributed among the four candidates in 1824.

Task

Students fill in missing information on the chart.

Input

Refer to figures 5.1 and 5.2.

Metacognitive Discussion

At what point did you realize that you were going to solve this problem? After successfully completing this activity, did you reflect back on those moments when flawed thinking occurred? Can you identify the background for that flawed thinking and why it was in error? How can you avoid repeating the same mistake in the future?

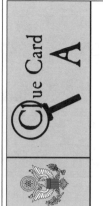

Clue Card A

1. Each candidate—Tennessee's Jackson, Virginia's Crawford, Kentucky's Clay, and Massachusetts's Adams—won all the electoral votes of his home state.
2. Delaware, Missouri, Illinois, and Mississippi had only the minimum number of electoral votes.
3. Adams won the electoral votes of all six New England states.
4. Jackson won the New Jersey and Pennsylvania electoral votes.
5. From the South, Jackson won all the electoral votes from the Carolinas as well as 11 out of a possible 13 electoral votes from the three Deep South states.

Clue Card B

1. For each 45,000 people in a state, there was one member of the U.S. House of Representatives.
2. A state's electoral votes equal its number of members of the U.S. House of Representatives added to the number of its U.S. senators.
3. In 1824, Massachusetts, North Carolina, Kentucky, and Ohio had the same number of electoral votes.
4. The New England states of Maine, New Hampshire, and Vermont are neighbors of Massachusetts.
5. John Adams did not receive a single vote—popular or electoral—from the state of Ohio.
6. Mississippi is a Deep South state bordered by Alabama and Louisiana.

Clue Card C

1. New Jersey, New Hampshire, and Connecticut had the same number of electoral votes.
2. Your task is to fill in the missing information on the chart.
3. The total number of popular votes cast in the presidential election of 1824 was 356,000.
4. Jackson received three of Louisiana's electoral votes, but Crawford and Clay were shut out.
5. Rather than give all their electoral votes to only one candidate, Maryland, Illinois, New York, Delaware, and Louisiana divided their electoral votes among the candidates.

Clue Card D

1. Neighbors in the New England region are Massachusetts, Rhode Island, and Connecticut.
2. Clay won all the electoral votes of only three states—Kentucky, Ohio, and Missouri.
3. In 19 states, the entire number of electoral votes went to the candidate who was the winner of the state's popular election.
4. Crawford had twice as many of Delaware's electoral votes as Adams, and the same could be said of Jackson in Illinois's electoral race with Adams.
5. Georgia is a Southern, but not Deep South, state.
6. Crawford received all of Virginia's electoral votes.

SkyLight Training and Publishing Inc.

Electoral College Votes Cast in 1824 Presidential Election Worksheet

State	1820 Population Approximate	House Seats	Electoral Votes	Jackson	Adams	Crawford	Clay
Georgia				____	____	9	____
So. Carolina				11	____	____	____
No. Carolina							
Virginia		22					
Maryland				7	3	1	____
Delaware							
New Jersey		6					
Pennyslvania				28	____	____	____
New York				1	26	5	4
Massachusetts							
Rhode Island					4		
New Hampshire							
Connecticut							
Missouri							
Maine				____	9	____	____
Alabama				5	____	____	____
Illinois							
Mississippi							
Indiana				5	____	____	____
Louisiana			5				
Ohio	585,000						
Tennessee		9					
Kentucky							
Vermont							
TOTAL			261		84	41	

Figure 5.1

SkyLight Training and Publishing Inc.

Electoral College Votes Cast in 1824 Presidential Election Answers

State	1820 Population Approximate	House Seats	Electoral Votes	Jackson	Adams	Crawford	Clay
Georgia		7	9	_____	_____	9	_____
So. Carolina		9	11	11	_____	_____	_____
No. Carolina		13	15	15	_____	_____	_____
Virginia		22	24	_____	_____	24	_____
Maryland		9	11	7	3	1	_____
Delaware		1	3	_____	1	2	_____
New Jersey		6	8	8	_____	_____	_____
Pennyslvania		26	28	_____	_____	_____	_____
New York		34	36	1	26	5	4
Massachusetts		13	15	_____	15	_____	_____
Rhode Island		2	4	_____	4	_____	_____
New Hampshire		6	8	_____	8	_____	_____
Connecticut		6	8	_____	8	_____	_____
Missouri		1	3	_____	_____	_____	_____
Maine		7	9	_____	_____	_____	_____
Alabama		3	5	5	_____	_____	_____
Illinois		1	3	2	1	_____	_____
Mississippi		1	3	3	_____	_____	_____
Indiana		3	5	5	_____	_____	_____
Louisiana		3	5	3	2	_____	_____
Ohio	585,000	15	15	_____	_____	_____	15
Tennessee		9	11	11	_____	_____	_____
Kentucky		13	15	_____	_____	_____	15
Vermont		5	7	_____	7	_____	_____
TOTAL		215	261	99	84	41	37

Figure 5.2

SkyLight Training and Publishing Inc.

The 1850s

Activity 39

Students increase their understanding of events leading to the Civil War.

Background Information

To prepare the teams, teachers may employ the jigsaw strategy, whereby all students drawing A cards huddle to review their information, and students drawing B, C, and D cards respectively do the same, before regrouping in the usual A-B-C-D team structure.

To prevent guessing, teachers should limit the number of times they check a team's work.

Objective

Students create a historian's tool, the time line, in order to understand events leading up to the Civil War.

Task

Students organize a time line of eight events.

Input

Compromise of 1850; publication of *Uncle Tom's Cabin*–1852; Kansas-Nebraska Act–1854; Bleeding Kansas–1856; Dred Scott decision–March 1857; Sumner-Brooks Affair–May 1857; Lincoln-Douglas Debates–1858; Harper's Ferry–1859.

Metacognitive Discussion

Did you borrow skills from a prior experience to complete this activity? Do you feel that you can always work through problems of this nature? Before you actually tackled the assignment, did you lay out plans for solving the problem? Is it a necessary thing, a good thing, or the best thing to map out everything beforehand? What would you do if a problem suddenly emerged and you had a short time to solve it?

SkyLight Training and Publishing Inc.

Clue Card A

1. The admission of California as a free state touched off a controversy that lasted for nine months and finally was settled by compromise.
2. Early in the decade, Harriet Beecher Stowe wrote and published a controversial novel, *Uncle Tom's Cabin.*
3. The unorganized territory of the Great Plains became the focal point for another antislavery-proslavery debate.
4. One year after passage of the Kansas-Nebraska Act, Nebraska voted to become a "free territory"; emphasis then shifted to Kansas, which became a battleground over the slavery issue.
5. John Brown led a revenge-seeking raid on Pottawatomie, Kansas, which would leave five proslavers dead. Three years later Brown would surface again in Virginia.
6. Just prior to the celebrated debates of Stephen Douglas and Abraham Lincoln the U.S. Supreme Court received a case concerning the status of slavery. This case came on the heels of the tensions and violence of the Great Plains.
7. Finally, according to the Courts, once a territory became a state, the state and not the Congress could determine whether slavery could exist.
8. Lincoln gained national prominence form his role in the great debates.
9. Seven years following the publication of *Uncle Tom's Cabin,* John Brown tried to start a slave rebellion in Virginia. This event would go into the time of the next presidential election.
10. Charles Sumner, a U.S. Senator and abolitionist, made a speech attacking slavery proponents.

Clue Card B

1. Southerners wanted to divide California into two states, one free and one slave, but antislavery forces opposed this option.
2. A novel portraying the cruelties of slavery sold over 300,000 copies in its first year.
3. Stephen Douglas proposed legistation that would divide the Great Plains into two territories, Kansas and Nebraska.
4. A Missouri slave named Dred Scott sued for his freedom in the Courts because he had once lived in free territory and felt a return to slave territory should not return him to slave status.
5. Abraham Lincoln challenged Stephen Douglas, Democrat, in the Illinois senatorial race.
6. John Brown and eighteen followers attacked the federal arsenal at Harper's Ferry, hoping to capture weapons and to atract revolting slaves.
7. Sumner made sneering personal references to the senator from South Carolina, Andrew P. Butler.
8. Those who traveled to California looking for gold were called "49ers."
9. Republicans unsuccessfully ran their first presidential candidate in 1856 (six years after California became a state).
10. The opponents who were upset over passage of Douglas' Kansas-Nebraska Act formed the Republican party.

SkyLight Training and Publishing Inc.

Clue Card D

1. Douglas and Lincoln debated in seven Illinois towns and attracted national press coverage.
2. Lincoln forced Douglas into admitting that Popular Sovereignty could work against slavery . . . this admission cost Douglas Southern support and ruined his presidential aspirations.
3. Stowe was the sister of Northern abolitionist Henry Ward Beecher.
4. The Court ruled that slaves were not citizens, so the U.S. Constitution did not apply to them.
5. One of the ingredients of the compromise was that the Utah and New Mexico territories would have no restrictions on slavery.
6. John Brown's attack failed and he had to surrender to a Colonel Robert E. Lee of the United States Army.
7. Douglas proposed scrapping the Missouri Compromise in favor of Popular Sovereignty, which promoted the process of allowing the people that lived in the territory to determine whether they would permit slavery.
8. Henry Ward Beecher, Northern clergyman and abolitionist, raised money to send boxes marked "Bibles" to anti-slavery forces in Kansas. However, instead of Bibles the boxes contained rifles and they were nicknamed "Beecher's Bibles."
9. Three days later Butler's nephew, Congressman Preston S. Brooks, approached Sumner at his desk and demanded an apology for the remarks he had made about his uncle.
10. Lincoln was the first Republican president, elected in 1860.

Clue Card C

1. Gold was discovered in California in 1848; due to the huge westward migration California would be ready for statehood in two years.
2. Stowe's book touched thousands who heretofore had no sentiments about slavery—pro or con.
3. The North thought Brooks a typical Southern thug while Southern sympathizers sent him dozens of canes imploring him to "put 'em to good use."
4. Popular sovereignty would determine the slavery matter until the U.S. Supreme Court settled the issue with a ruling in 1857.
5. Thousands of pro-slavery Missourians crossed the border to stuff the ballot box on territorial election day; election results were considered tainted by many and valid by others.
6. The Court also said slaves were considered "chattel" or property and the Constitution protected the property rights of the slave owners.
7. Six weeks after his surrender, John Brown was tried and convicted for treason. He was hanged and instantly became a martyr in the North. The South was stunned by the Northern reaction over Brown.
8. Sumner would not apologize and Brooks beat him into unconsciousness with a cane he brought with him for the occasion.
9. The Republican party, an anti-slavery party, defeated 35 of the 42 Northern Democrats who had voted for the Kansas-Nebraska Act in its first year of existence in 1854.

The Roaring Twenties

Activity 40

Students explore the chronology of events in the 1920s.

Objective

Students learn to create a historian's tool, a time line.

Task

Students create a time line of ten events.

Input

Red Scare arrests begin–June 1919; Prohibition begins–October 1919; KDKA–November 1920, Scopes Trial–1925, Lindbergh Flight–May 1927, Execution of Sacco and Vanzetti–August 1927; Teapot Dome Scandal verdict–October 1927; the film *The Jazz Singer*–December 1927, St. Valentine's Day Massacre–February 1929, Stock Market Crash–October 1929.

Metacognitive Discussion

Why is making a time line useful? In what other subjects will the ability to order events chronologically be useful?

Clue Card A

1. The popular automobile of the decade was Henry Ford's Model T, nicknamed the "Tin Lizzie."
2. The first radio east of the Mississippi River began operation as it transmitted the results of the Harding-Cox presidential race at the start of the decade. Its call letters began with the letter K, although the call letters for all radio stations later established west of the Mississippi began with the letter W.
3. Al Jolson starred in the first talking motion picture, which began to play in theaters in December of the same year as a historical achievement in aviation. The motion picture, called a "talkie," was about a musical performer.
4. Jazz and lively dancing were popular in the 1920s. The "Charleston" was a popular energetic dance that was easy to learn.

Clue Card B

1. In October 1919, Congress passed the Volstead Act, which forbade the sale or use of liquor. This year started the period in which Americans chose either to abstain from using alcohol or to drink "home brew," "bathtub gin," "rot gut," "hooch," "bootleg gin," or "moonshine" illegally.
2. The Tennessee legislature passed a law stating that the Book of Genesis should serve as the only source for an explanation of the creation of human beings. The jury for the trial held in the local court agreed with the legislature in this mid-decade trial that challenged this contention. Over the presiding judge's bench was a ten-foot banner with the words "Read Your Bible."
3. On the time line, list the following: The Jazz Singer, KDKA, Lindbergh Flight, Execution of Sacco and Vanzetti, Prohibition begins, Red Scare arrests begin, Scopes Trial, Stock Market Crash, Teapot Dome Scandal verdict, and St. Valentine's Day Massacre.
4. The spirit of the decade abruptly deflated after thousands of investors were ruined on this day in October 1929.

Clue Card C

1. At its height during the decade, the Ku Klux Klan boasted of having five million members. Its message was "Kill Kikes, Koons, and Katholics."
2. Your task is to create a time line. Draw a line and, alongside it, write each of the ten events and its date in chronological order.
3. Cupid was not the only one shooting on this day in 1929 when seven crime syndicate members were killed in Chicago.
4. Three years before the decade ended, Charles Lindbergh landed in Paris after making the first transatlantic flight in his plane *The Spirit of St. Louis.*
5. African-American writers enjoyed popularity during this period, which was known as "The Harlem Renaissance."

Clue Card D

1. Two immigrants had been convicted of a crime in Massachusetts and sentenced to death despite evidence that cast a reasonable doubt as to their guilt. The execution was carried out six years later, in August of the same year Jolson and Lindbergh made headlines and the U.S. Supreme Court invalidated certain Wyoming oil leases.
2. Four months before the Volstead Act was passed, U.S. Attorney General Mitchell Palmer instituted arrests of sympathizers with the 1917 Bolshevik Revolution. Over 5,000 people in 33 cities were arrested in less than a year for "support of the reds."
3. Three years into the decade, Washington was rocked with scandals. The biggest scandal involved an "oily smudge" that "leaked" out over lands in Wyoming.
4. Trouble "brewed" when rumors of illegal oil leases in Wyoming began to circulate in 1924.
5. A member of Warren G. Harding's staff had the dubious distinction of being the first member of a presidential administration to be jailed.

What's in a Name?

Activity 41

Students review an American history course in terms of presidents.

Objective

Students review major issues of American presidents' terms and reflect on how history as well as popular culture record the presidents' effects on American life and government.

Task

Students match each U.S. president with the nickname(s) that have been associated with that president.

Input

George Washington–Old Fox; John Adams–Old Sink or Swim; Thomas Jefferson–Pen of the Revolution; James Madison–Father of the Constitution; James Monroe–Last of the Cocked Hats; John Quincy Adams–Old Man Eloquent; Andrew Jackson–Old Hickory; Martin Van Buren–Little Magician; William Henry Harrison–Tippecanoe; John Tyler–His Accidency; James K. Polk–Napoleon of the Stump; Zachary Taylor–Old Rough and Ready; Millard Fillmore–the American Louis Philippe; Franklin Pierce–Handsome Frank; James Buchanan–Old Buck; Abraham Lincoln–Honest Abe, the Great Emancipator; Andrew Johnson–Sir Veto; Ulysses S. Grant–Uncle Sam; Rutherford B. Hayes–His Fraudulency; James A. Garfield–the Preacher President; Chester A. Arthur–Elegant Arthur; Grover Cleveland–Buffalo Hangman, Uncle Jumbo; Benjamin Harrison–Little Ben; Grover Cleveland–Buffalo Hangman, Uncle Jumbo; William McKinley–Wobbly

Willie; Theodore Roosevelt–the Great White Chief; William H. Taft–(no nickname); Woodrow Wilson–the Professor; Warren G. Harding–(no nickname); Calvin Coolidge–Silent Cal; Herbert Hoover–Chief; Franklin Delano Roosevelt–FDR, the Boss; Harry S Truman–Give 'em Hell Harry; Dwight D. Eisenhower–Ike; John F. Kennedy–JFK; Lyndon Baines Johnson–LBJ; Richard M. Nixon–Tricky Dick; Gerald R. Ford–Junie; James E. Carter–Jimmy; Ronald Reagan–the Gipper; George Bush–Poppy; William Clinton–Slick Willie.

Metacognitive Discussion

Did you think this would be a difficult task or an easy task when you first viewed the assignment? What did you think would be the first step to take in order to complete the assignment? Did you need to do anything else in order to understand the activity?

1. Our first president's nickname was "Old Fox."
2. "Old Man Eloquent" fell between the "Last of the Cocked Hats" and "Old Hickory."
3. The "Great White Chief" was the youngest president.
4. The two Democratic presidents between "Ike" and "Tricky Dick" were known simply by their initials.
5. "Old Rough and Ready" was a hero in the Mexican War.
6. "Junie" was the first vice-president who came to the office because of a president's resignation.
7. "Tippecanoe" died one month after taking office.
8. Millard Fillmore, successor to "Old Rough and Ready," was known as "the American Louis Philippe."
9. After the first two presidents served, the "Pen of the Revolution" was elected to his term.
10. Our forty-second president was nicknamed "Slick Willie."
11. "Little Ben" was president between the two terms of the "Buffalo Hangman."
12. Eisenhower fought in WWI and was a World War II hero.

1. "His Accidency" became president after serving as vice-president for only one year.
2. "Honest Abe" also was known as "the Great Emancipator."
3. James Polk wanted to annex Texas; he is known for promoting the concept of Manifest Destiny.
4. Teddy Roosevelt was the youngest president in history.
5. Gerald Ford was appointed to the vice-presidency after Spiro Agnew resigned as vice-president. Ford succeeded to the presidency when Richard Nixon ("Tricky Dick") resigned from office.
6. Zachary Taylor fought in the Mexican War (1846–1848).
7. "Old Hickory," also known as Andrew Jackson, was the first president from the West, actually from Tennessee—then considered the "West."
8. "Old Sink or Swim" followed "Old Hickory."
9. "Handsome Frank" was president between "the American Louis Philippe" and "Old Buck."
10. "Tricky Dick" was the thirty-seventh president of the United States.
11. "Give 'em Hell Harry" had to finish FDR's fourth term in office. (FDR was the only president elected for a fourth consecutive term.)

Figure 2.4

Clue Card C

1. Manifest Destiny is synonymous with the "Napoleon of the Stump."
2. William Henry Harrison caught a cold on Inauguration Day and only lived a month into his presidency.
3. "Jimmy" lost his reelection bid to an older man called the "Gipper."
4. "Uncle Sam" was a Civil War hero.
5. The "Buffalo Hangman" was the only person to serve two nonconsecutive presidential terms.
6. The "Great White Chief" replaced "Wobbly Willie" after the assassination.
7. "His Fraudulency" followed "Uncle Sam."
8. "Sir Veto" took office when Lincoln was assassinated.
9. William Taft did not have a nickname although he had a long public life. He served both as President and as Chief Justice of the United States Supreme Court.
10. Roaring Twenties president Warren G. Harding did not have any recorded nicknames.
11. Sensibly, the "Pen of the Revolution" preceded the "Father of the Constitution."

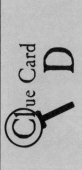

Clue Card D

1. "Ike" was a hero in WW II.
2. The "Boss" was elected to an unprecedented four terms.
3. "The Professor" fell between two nicknameless presidents.
4. The "Chief" directly preceded "the Boss."
5. The "Preacher President" followed "His Fraudulency."
6. "Elegant Arthur" was president right before the "Buffalo Hangman," who also was known as "Uncle Jumbo."
7. "Silent Cal" was succeeded by the "Chief."
8. "Poppy" succeeded the "Gipper" as president.
9. Ulysses S. Grant was a Civil War hero.
10. James Carter was known as "Jimmy."
11. "Wobbly Willie" was assassinated shortly into his second term.
12. The "Little Magician" followed "Old Hickory."

Five Great Presidents

Activity 42

Students review American history coursework and historians' opinions.

Background Information

Some historians and political scientists who studied the American presidents have produced lists of the five, ten, or other numbers of presidents they personally would rank as the "greatest" presidents. This activity is based the results of a 1995 survey of 168 historians on the historical ranking of American presidents.

Objective

Students understand subjectivity of and rationale for lists of "greatest" or "best" presidents.

Task

Students rank selected presidents from best to fifth best according to some historians' personal views of the five best U.S. presidents.

Input

Franklin D. Roosevelt–1, Abraham Lincoln–2, Theodore Roosevelt–3, George Washington–4, Thomas Jefferson–5.

Metacognitive Discussion

What are some methods for determining excellence? What are the methods historians should use in determining excellence in presidents? How can you use standards of excellence in studying in a class?

Clue Card A

1. George Washington took office with no one to serve as a model or guide.
2. If all of the presidents were alive today, the fourth-rated president would be the oldest of the great presidents.
3. Franklin Delano Roosevelt generally hid from the public the fact he was confined to a wheelchair.
4. One of the great presidents had a stuffed animal named after him.

Clue Card B

1. At the time of his election, Washington was the most popular and influential man in America.
2. Not one of these great presidents was born in the twentieth century.
3. Lincoln was shot in the Ford Theater in Washington, D.C., while attending a play.

Clue Card C

1. Two presidents with the same last name were separated by the second-greatest president.
2. With the secession of the eleven Southern states, Abraham Lincoln faced one of the most perplexing problems of any president.
3. Thomas Jefferson is considered the "brainiest" of all the presidents who have held the office.
4. From the information given in the clues, determine the order of the presidents from 1 to 5, with 1 being the "greatest" in the view of some historians.

Clue Card D

1. If you had four coins totaling 41 cents, the third-rated president would not be portrayed on any of the coins.
2. Thomas Jefferson (who followed Washington in the ratings) had to backtrack on his principle of strict interpretation of the Constitution in order to purchase the Louisiana Territory.
3. FDR's program to combat the Great Depression was called the New Deal.
4. The youngest of the great presidents to hold the office led a military unit nick-named the "Rough Riders."

Index

SkyLight
Training and Publishing Inc.

We Prepare Your Teachers Today
for the Classrooms of Tomorrow

Learn from Our Books and from Our Authors!

Ignite Learning in Your School or District.

SkyLight's team of classroom-experienced consultants can help you foster systemic change for increased student achievement.

Professional development is a process, not an event. SkyLight's seasoned practitioners drive the creation of our on-site professional development programs, graduate courses, research-based publications, interactive video courses, teacher-friendly training materials, and online resources—call SkyLight Training and Publishing Inc. today.

SkyLight specializes in three professional development areas.

Specialty # **1** **Best Practices**

We **model** the best practices that result in improved student performance and guided applications.

Specialty # **2** **Making the Innovations Last**

We help set up **support** systems that make innovations part of everyday practice in the long-term systemic improvement of your school or district.

Specialty # **3** **How to Assess the Results**

We prepare your school leaders to encourage and **assess** teacher growth, **measure** student achievement, and **evaluate** program success.

Contact the SkyLight team and begin a process toward long-term results.

SkyLight
Training and Publishing Inc.

2626 S. Clearbrook Dr., Arlington Heights, IL 60005
800-348-4474 • 847-290-6600 • FAX 847-290-6609
http://www.iriskylight.com

There are

one-story intellects,

two-story intellects, and three-story

intellects with skylights. All fact collectors, who

have no aim beyond their facts, are one-story men. Two-story men

compare, reason, generalize, using the labors of the fact collectors as

well as their own. Three-story men idealize, imagine,

predict—their best illumination comes from

above, through the skylight.

—Oliver Wendell

Holmes